The Seagull

When it opened in St Petersburg in 1896, *The Seagull* survived only five performances after a disastrous first night. Two years later it was revived by Stanislavsky at the newly-founded Moscow Arts Theatre and was an immediate success. The first of Chekhov's four masterpieces that changed forever the nature and possibilities of drama, *The Seagull* was followed by *Uncle Vanya* (1899), *Three Sisters* (1901) and *The Cherry Orchard* in 1904, the year of Chekhov's death.

Michael Frayn, who is both proficient in Russian and a playwright himself, is the ideal translator; the familiar Chekhovian characters are reborn in beautiful idiomatic English that permits the modern reader to appreciate more than ever before the qualities of the original. For this edition Michael Frayn has also provided a full introduction and a chronology of Chekhov's life and works.

The front cover photograph shows Robert Stephens (Gayev) in the National Theatre production (1978) and was taken by Zöe Dominic. The photograph of Chekhov on the back cover is reproduced by courtesy of the Radio Times Hulton Picture Library.

Methuen's Theatre Classics

Anton Chekhov

THE SEAGULL

A comedy in Four Acts

Translated and introduced by
MICHAEL FRAYN

A Methuen Paperback

891.72
C4gc
1986
c. 1

...N THEATRE CLASSIC

...slation first published
...eat Britain in 1986
...ethuen London Ltd,
11 New Fetter Lane, London EC4P 4EE
Published in the United States of America
by Methuen Inc,
29 West 35th Street, New York, NY 10001
Translation copyright © 1986 by Michael Frayn
Introduction and chronology copyright © 1986
by Michael Frayn
Photoset – Plantin by 🌂 Tek-Art, Croydon, Surrey
Printed in Great Britain

British Library Cataloguing in Publication Data

Chekhov, A. P.
    The seagull: a comedy in four acts.——(Methuen's theatre classics)
    I. Title   II. Frayn, Michael   III. Chaïka. *English*
    891.72'3   PG3456.C5

    ISBN 0-413-42140-6

CAUTION

All rights whatsoever in this play are strictly reserved and
application for performance etc., should be made to
Fraser & Dunlop (Scripts) Ltd, 91 Regent St, London
W1R 8RU. No performance may be given unless a licence
has been obtained.

This paperback is sold subject to the condition that it shall
not, by way of trade or otherwise, be lent, resold, hired
out, or otherwise circulated without the publisher's prior
consent in any form of binding or cover other than that
in which it is published and without a similar condition
including this condition being imposed on the subsequent
purchaser.

REDFORD BRANCH
21200 GRAND RIVER. 48219

APR '89

RD

Anton Chekhov

1860   Born the son of a grocer and grandson of a serf, in Taganrog, a small port on the Sea of Azov, where he spends his first nineteen years, and which he describes on a return visit in later life as 'Asia, pure and simple!'

1875   His father, bankrupt, flees from Taganrog concealed beneath a mat at the bottom of a cart.

1876   A former lodger buys the Chekhov's house and puts the rest of the family out.

1879   Chekhov rejoins his family, who have followed his father to Moscow, and enrols at the university to study medicine.

1880   Begins contributing humorous material to minor magazines under the pen-name Antosha Chekhonte.

1882   Begins contributing regularly to the St. Petersburg humorous journal *Oskolki* – short stories and sketches, and a column on Moscow life.

1884   Qualifies as a doctor, and begins practising in Moscow – the start of a sporadic second career which over the years brings him much hard work but little income.

1885   Begins writing for the *St. Petersburg Gazette*, which gives him the opportunity to break out of the tight restrictions on length and the rigidly humorous format in which he has worked up to now.

1886   Another step up the journalistic ladder – he begins writing, under his own name and for good money, for *Novoye vremya*. Alexei Suvorin, its millionaire proprietor, an anti-Semitic reactionary who had the concession on all the railway bookstands in Russia, becomes Chekhov's close friend.

1887   Is a literary success in St. Petersburg. Writes *Ivanov* as a result of a commission from a producer who wants a light entertainment in the Chekhonte style. The play is produced in Moscow (his first production) to a mixture of clapping and hissing.

1888   Begins to publish his stories in the 'thick journals'; has survived his career in comic journalism to emerge as a serious and respectable writer. But at the same time begins writing four one-act farces for the theatre.

1889   *The Wood Demon* (which Chekhov later uses as raw material for *Uncle Vanya*) opens at a second-rate Moscow theatre, and survives for only three performances.

1890   Makes the appalling journey across Siberia (largely in unsprung carts over unsurfaced roads) to visit and report on the penal colony on the island of Sakhalin. Sets out to interview the entire population of prisoners and exiles, at the rate of 160 a day.

1892   Travels the back country of Nizhny Novgorod and Voronyezh provinces in the middle of winter, trying to prevent a recurrence of the previous year's famine among the peasants. Is banqueted by the provincial governors. Moves to the modest but comfortable estate he had bought himself at Melikhovo, fifty miles south of Moscow. Becomes an energetic and enlightened landowner, cultivating the soil and doctoring the peasants. Spends three months organizing the district against an expected cholera epidemic.

1894   Starts work on the first of the three schools he builds in the Melikhovo district.

1896   *The Seagull* opens in St. Petersburg, and survives only five performances after a disastrous first night. Chekhov tells Suvorin he won't have another play put on even if he lives another seven hundred years.

1897   Suffers a violent lung haemorrhage while dining with Suvorin, and is forced to recognize at last what he has long closed his eyes to – that he is suffering from advanced consumption. (Is also constantly plagued by piles, gastritis, migraine, dizzy spells, and palpitations of the heart.) Winters in Nice.

1898   Moves his headquarters to the Crimean warmth of Yalta. Stanislavsky revives *The Seagull* (with twelve weeks rehearsal) at the newly-founded Moscow Arts Theatre, and it is an immediate success.

1899   Sells the copyright in all his works, past, present, and future, to the St. Petersburg publisher A. F. Marks – a contract which is to burden the rest of his life. *Uncle Vanya* produced successfully by the Moscow Arts Theatre.

1901   *Three Sisters* produced by the Moscow Arts Theatre, but rather poorly received. Chekhov marries his mistress, Olga Knipper, an actress in the Moscow Arts company, who was the original Arkadina in *The Seagull*, Yelena in *Uncle Vanya*, Masha in *Three Sisters* and Ranyevskaya in *The Cherry Orchard*.

1904   *The Cherry Orchard* is produced in January; and in July, after two heart attacks, Chekhov dies in a hotel bedroom in the German spa of Badenweiler.

Introduction

'A comedy – three f., six m., four acts, rural scenery (a view over a lake); much talk of literature, little action, five bushels of love.'

Chekhov's own synopsis of the play, in a letter to his friend Suvorin written a month before he finished it, is characteristically self-mocking and offhand. (His cast-list is even one f. short, unless he added the fourth woman only during that last month, or when he revised the play the following year). He says in the same letter that he is cheating against the conventions of the theatre, but no one could have begun to guess from his flippant resumé how extraordinary an event was being prepared for the world. No doubt Chekhov took the play more seriously than the letter suggests, but even he can scarcely have realised quite what he had on his hands: a catastrophe so grotesque that it made him swear never to write for the theatre again; a triumph so spectacular that it established him as a kind of theatrical saint; and the first of the four masterpieces that would change forever the nature and possibilities of drama.

Chekhov wrote *The Seagull* in 1895. He was 35 years old, and already an established and celebrated writer who had known almost nothing but success. But the success was on the printed page, as a writer of short stories, and the leap he was trying to make now, from page to stage, was one which few major writers have managed. He had written for the theatre before, of course. He had done a number of short plays, all but one broadly comic, and related to his humorous journalism rather than to his more serious work. He had also written at least three full-length plays with more serious intentions – the untitled piece of his student days, *Ivanov*, and *The Wood Demon* – and with these he had encountered almost the only setbacks of his career so far. Now, as he finished *The Seagull* and read it through, he had a moment of fundamental doubt about the direction he was trying to take. 'I am once again convinced', he wrote to Suvorin, 'that I am absolutely not a dramatist.'

There were prolonged difficulties in getting the play past the theatrical censor (see A Note on the Translation), which almost made him despair of the whole enterprise, but once this hurdle was behind him Chekhov's apparently offhand mood returned. The play was to be performed at the Alexandrinsky Theatre in St. Petersburg, where *Ivanov* had been well received seven years earlier after a highly disputed opening in Moscow, and his letters in September 1896, as rehearsals approached, have the same cheerful flippancy as his original account of the play to Suvorin. They read with hindsight as ironically as the banter of some doomed statesman as he goes all unknowing towards his assassination. To his brother Georgi: 'My play will be done in the Alexandrinsky Theatre at a jubilee benefit [for the actress Levkeyeva]. It will be a resounding gala occasion. Do come!' To his friend Shcheglov: 'Around the 6th [of October] the thirst for glory will draw me to the Palmyra of the north for the rehearsals of my *Seagull*.' To his brother Alexander: 'You are to meet me at the station, in full parade uniform (as laid down for a customs officer retd.) . . . On the 17th Oct my new play is being done at the Alexandrinsky. I would tell you what it's called, only I'm afraid you'll go round boasting you wrote it.'

The seventeenth, when it came, was indeed a resounding gala occasion. 'I have been going to the theatre in St. Petersburg for more than twenty years,' wrote a correspondent in a theatrical journal afterwards, 'and I have witnessed a great many "flops" . . . but I can remember nothing resembling what happened in the auditorium at Levkeyeva's 25th jubilee.' The trouble started within the first few minutes of Act One. Levkeyeva was a popular light comedy actress, and even though she had no part in the play the audience were minded to laugh. The first thing that struck them as funny was the sight of Masha offering a pinch of snuff to Medvedenko, and thereafter they laughed at everything. Konstantin's play, Konstantin with his head bandaged – it was all irresistible. By Act Two, according to the papers next day, the dialogue was beginning to be drowned by the noise and movement in the audience; by Act Three the hissing had become general and deafening. The reviewers struggled for superlatives to describe 'the grandiose scale' of the play's failure, the 'scandalous' and 'unprecedented' nature of 'such a dizzying flop, such a stunning fiasco.' The author, they reported, had fled from the theatre.

According to his own accounts of the evening Chekhov escaped from the theatre only when the play ended, after sitting out two or three acts in Levkeyeva's dressing-room, had supper at Romanov's, 'in the proper way', then slept soundly and caught the train home to Melikhovo next day. Even Suvorin accused him of cowardice in running away. All he had run away from, he protested in a letter to Suvorin's wife, was the intolerable sympathy of his friends. He told Suvorin: 'I behaved as reasonably and coolly as a man who has proposed and been refused, and who has no choice but to go away . . . Back in my own home I took a dose of castor oil, had a wash in cold water – and now I could sit down and write a new play.'

But Suvorin, with whom he was staying, recorded in his diary that Chekhov's first reaction had been to give up the theatre. He had not come back until two in the morning, when he told Suvorin that he had been walking about the streets, and that 'if I live another seven hundred years I shan't have a single play put on. Enough is enough. In this area I am a failure.' When he went home next day he left a note telling Suvorin to halt the printing of his plays, and saying that he would never forget the previous evening. He claimed to have slept well, and to be leaving 'in an absolutely tolerable frame of mind'; but he managed nevertheless to leave his dressing-gown and other belongings on the train, and the accounts he subsequently gave of the evening in various letters to friends and relations make it clear how painful the experience had been. 'The moral of all this', he wrote to his sister Masha, 'is that one shouldn't write plays.'

And yet, not much more than a month later, in another letter to Suvorin, he was mentioning the existence of a play 'not known to anyone in the world' – *Uncle Vanya*. By this time, too – in fact from the very next performance – the tide had turned at the Alexandrinsky. 'A total and unanimous success', wrote Komissarzhevskaya, who was playing Nina, in a letter to Chekhov after the second performance of *The Seagull*, 'such as it ought to be and could not but be.' And two years later, in a stunning reversal of fortune of the kind that occurs in plays (though never in Chekhov's own), it triumphed in Moscow as noisily as it had failed in Petersburg.

In fact the event went rather beyond anything one might find in a play; it was more like something out of a backstage musical – particularly as recounted by Stanislavsky (who was both directing and playing Trigorin) in his memoir of Chekhov. For a start the fate of the newly-founded Moscow Arts Theatre depended upon it. The other opening productions had mostly either failed or been banned by the Metropolitan of Moscow, and all hopes were now riding aboard this one salvaged wreck. There was a suitable love interest depending upon the outcome of the evening – the leading lady (Olga Knipper, playing Arkadina) and the author had just met, and were to marry two plays later – provided there *were* two more plays to allow their acquaintance to develop. Moreover, the author had now been diagnosed as consumptive and exiled to Yalta. The dress rehearsal was of course a disaster. At the end of it Chekhov's sister Masha arrived to express her horror at the prospect of what another failure like Petersburg would do to her sick brother, and they considered abandoning the production and closing the theatre.

When the curtain finally went up on the first night the audience was sparse, and the cast all reeked of the valerian drops they had taken to tranquillise themselves. As they reach the end of Act One Stanislavsky's paragraphs become shorter and shorter:

'We had evidently flopped. The curtain came down in the silence of the tomb. The actors huddled fearfully together and listened to the audience.

'It was as quiet as the grave.

'Heads emerged from the wings as the stage staff listened as well.

'Silence.

'Someone started to cry. Knipper was holding back hysterical sobs. We went offstage in silence.

'At that moment the audience gave a kind of moan and burst into applause. We rushed to take a curtain.

'People say that we were standing on stage with our backs half-turned to the audience, that we had terror on our faces, that none of us thought to bow and that someone was even sitting down. We had evidently not taken in what had happened.

'In the house the success was colossal; on stage it was like a second Easter. Everyone kissed everyone else, not excluding strangers who came bursting backstage. Someone went into hysterics. Many people, myself among them, danced a wild dance for joy and excitement.'

The only person who remained completely calm seems to have been Chekhov himself, since he was 800 miles away in the Crimea. But when after Act Three the audience began to shout 'Author! Author!', as audiences do in this kind of script, and Nemirovich-Danchenko explained to them that the author was not present, they shouted 'Send a telegram!' In the event he was informed of his triumph not only by telegram, but in shoals of letters from everyone present. But, judging by how rarely he referred to it either beforehand or afterwards in his own letters from Yalta, he had kept this production at a distance emotionally as well as geographically, and the Moscow success was considerably more remote from him than the Petersburg failure.

There were of course external reasons for the play's extraordinarily different reception in the two capitals. The choice of Levkeyeva's benefit night in St. Petersburg, on the one hand, and the fact that it had been produced there at nine days notice; the thorough preparation in Moscow on the other hand, with twelve weeks' rehearsal. The Moscow audience may also have been impressed by the sheer weight of Stanislavsky's production. At the beginning of Act One, for example, his prompt copy notes: 'Glimmer of lantern, distant singing of drunk, distant howling of dog, croaking of frogs, cry of corncrake, intermittent strokes of distant church bell . . . summer lightning, barely audible far-off thunder . . .' – All this before the first two characters have even got on stage. Chekhov, grateful as he was for the success, was ungratefully cool about the production when he finally saw it. He greatly disliked the slowness of Stanislavsky's tempo, and according to Nemirovich-Danchenko he threatened to put a stage-direction in his next play saying: 'The action takes place in a country where there are no mosquitoes or crickets or other insects that interfere with people's conversations.'

Even without Levkeyeva or the corncrakes, though, the play would almost certainly have elicited a passionate response of one kind or another. Its influence has been so widespread and pervasive since that it is difficult now to realise what a departure it was. The traditional function of literature in general, and of drama in particular, has always been to simplify and formalise the confused world of our experience; to isolate particular emotions and states of mind from the flux of feeling in which we live; to make our conflicts coherent; to illustrate values and to impose a moral (and therefore human) order upon a non-moral and inhuman universe; to make intention visible, and to suggest the process by which it takes effect. *The Seagull* is a critical survey of this function. For a start two of the characters are writers. One of them is using the traditional techniques without questioning them, one of them is searching for some even more formalised means of expression; and what interests Chekhov is how life eludes the efforts of both of them. Konstantin cannot even begin to capture it, for all the seriousness of his intentions; Trigorin feels that in the end all he has ever managed to do without falsity is landscapes, while his obsessive need to write drains his experience of all meaning apart from its literary possibilities. The extraordinary trick of the play is that all around the two writers we see the very life that they are failing to capture. What Chekhov is doing, in fact, is something formally impossible – to look behind the simplification and formalisation by which the world is represented in art and to show the raw, confused flux of the world itself, where nothing has its moral value written upon it, or for that matter its cause or its effect, or even its boundaries or its identity.

The most obvious characteristic of this approach is the play's ambiguity of tone. The author does not give us any of the customary indications as to whether we are to find these events comic or tragic. Indeed, what we are watching has not even been clearly organised into *events*; a lot of it bears a striking resemblance to the non-events out of which the greater part of out life consists. Then again, the play is to a quite astonishing extent morally neutral. It displays no moral conflict and takes up no moral attitude to its characters. Even now, after all these years, some people still find this difficult to accept. They talk as if Arkadina and Trigorin, at any rate, were monsters, and as if the point of the play were to expose her egotism and his spinelessness. It is indeed impossible not to be appalled by Arkadina's insensitivity towards her son, or by the ruthlessness with which she attempts to keep Trigorin attached to her; moral neutrality is not moral blindness. But Konstantin continues to find good in her, for all his jealousy and irritation, and she remains capable of inspiring the love of those around her. Konstantin's assessment is just as valid as ours; the devotion of Dorn and Shamrayev is just as real and just as important as our outrage. There is moral irony, too, in her manipulation of Trigorin; had she succeeded more completely in blackmailing him to remain with her she might have saved Nina from the misery that engulfs her. It is hard to respect Trigorin as we see him crumble in Arkadina's hands, harder still to like him when we know how he has treated Nina. But Masha likes and respects him, and for good reason – because he listens to her and takes her seriously; no grounds are offered for discounting her judgment. And when Trigorin wanders back in the last act, makes his peace with Konstantin, and settles down to lotto with the others, he is once again neither good nor bad in their eyes, in spite of what he has done; he is at that moment just a man who always seems to come out on top, whether in lotto or in love. We are perfectly entitled to find against him, of course – but that is our own verdict; there has been no direction to the jury in the judge's summing-up; indeed, no summing-up and no judge.

But then nothing is fixed. Everything is open to interpretation. Are we, for instance, to take Konstantin seriously as a writer? Impossible, after Nina's complaint that there are no living creatures in his work. But then it turns out that Dorn likes it, and he is a man of robust good sense (though not good enough to prevent his ruining Polina's life). And in Act Four we discover that Konstantin is at any rate good enough to be able to make a career as a professional writer. But even then Trigorin's judgment remains the same as Nina's, and Konstantin comes round to much the same view himself.

No one is valued for us; nothing is firmly located or fully explained. Why is Arkadina called Arkadina? She is Sorina by birth and Trepleva by marriage. It could be a stage-name, of course, or she could have married more than once. The people around her presumably know. They do not trouble to tell us. Has Dorn had an affair with Arkadina in the past? Is this why Polina is so relentlessly jealous of her? Is it what Arkadina is referring to when she talks about how irresistible he had been in the past? (In an earlier draft Polina begins to weep quietly at this point; but that may of course be for the lost early days of her own love.) In an astonishing moment at the end of Act One we do in fact stumble across one of the unexplained secrets of this world, when Dorn snatches Masha's snuff-box away from her, admonishes her for her 'filthy habit', and flings it into the bushes. From that one gesture of licensed impatience, without a word being said, we understand why Masha feels nothing for her father, why she sees herself as being 'of dubious descent', and why she feels so close to Dorn; because Dorn is her father, not Shamrayev. But who knows this, apart from us and Dorn? Not Masha herself, apparently. Does Shamrayev? Arkadina? Medvedenko? We are not told; the clouds that have parted for a moment close in again.

But then which of them knows about Dorn's relationship with Masha's mother in the first place? Perhaps everyone; or perhaps no one. We can only speculate. In any case it is characteristic of the relationships in the play; overt or covert, they are all one-sided, unsatisfactory, anomalous, and unlikely ever to be resolved. Medvedenko loves Masha who loves Konstantin who loves Nina who loves Trigorin who is supposed to love Arkadina, but who doesn't really love anyone, not even himself. No one's life can be contained in the forms that marriage and family offer. Konstantin's dissatisfaction with the existing dramatic forms is only a special case of this general condition. Plainly Chekhov is not advocating new social forms, in the way that Konstantin is calling for new literary ones. In the end even Konstantin comes to think that it is not a question of forms, old or new – the important thing is to write from the heart; nor are there any social forms suggested in the play which could ever contain the great flux of life itself.

We cannot help wondering, of course, if in this play we for once catch a glimpse of its elusive author. Chekhov is astonishingly absent from his works. Even the most intimately understood of his characters is unlike him – from quite different backgrounds, most of them, with quite different feelings and outlooks. But here is a play about two professional writers; it is unlikely that it does not reflect his own experience in some way. Konstantin is scarcely a plausible candidate, overwhelmed as he is by an artistic family, obsessed by questions of literary theory, and unable to create a living character; Chekhov's parents, after all, ran a provincial grocery, he displayed no interest in theory, and life is the very quality in which his stories and plays abound. But Trigorin is another matter. He is a celebrated and successful author, in much the same way that Chekhov was. His passion is fishing; so was Chekhov's. His modest estimate of his place in Russian letters is very much the kind of thing that Chekhov might have said mockingly about himself. More importantly, it seems at any rate plausible that his painful memories of beginning his career, and the terrible compulsion to write which is eating his life, reflect something that Chekhov felt about himself – particularly since the only palliative for his obsession is fishing. But this is about as far as we can push the parallel. David Magarshack, in his book *The Real Chekhov*, goes on to suppose that Trigorin is Chekhov's spokeman, and that when he tells Nina about the need he feels to pronounce on social questions he is making some kind of declaration of social commitment on Chekhov's behalf. This is preposterous. Trigorin is not even issuing a manifesto on his own behalf – he is making a confession of helplessness and ineptitude. Chekhov was notorious for refusing to pronounce on social questions, and if there is any manifesto in *The Seagull* it is plainly its general orientation *against* the imposition of the author's own interpretations and views upon his material.

Any biographical parallel has in any case clearly broken down by this point. There would be something characteristically self-mocking in choosing a second-rate author to represent himself, but when Trigorin says finally that all he can write is landscapes we realise that the picture which has been built up deliberately excludes the very essence of Chekhov's literary identity. Nor do any of the other biographical details fit. Arkadina is indeed based in part upon an actress, Yavorkskaya, who seems from her letters to have been very briefly his mistress. But Chekhov, unlike Trigorin, had no difficulty in disentangling himself from her, and in keeping women at arm's length generally. One of the women who were in love with Chekhov, Lika Mizinova, he kept at bay so successfully that she provided a model for not one but two of the characters in *The Seagull*: first Masha, with her life ruined by the unquenchable but unreciprocated love she has for Konstantin, and then Nina. To forget the Masha-like feelings she had for Chekhov, Lika threw herself into a disastrous affair with a friend of his, the Ukrainian writer Potapenko, who left his wife and went off to Paris with Lika, where he made her pregnant and then abandoned her. Potapenko, ironically, having provided Chekhov with a model for the more dubious aspects of Trigorin, was then called upon by him, after the play was finished, to undertake all the endless negotiations with the censor for him.

Nina was also contributed to by another of Chekhov's admirers, the writer Lidia Avilova, whom he treated even more high-handedly. She gave him a charm for his watch-chain with a page reference inscribed upon it, exactly as Nina does Trigorin with the medallion, and referring to a passage in one of Chekhov's stories which is exactly the same as the passage in Trigorin's works referred to by Nina's present – 'If ever you have need of my life, then come and take it'. Meeting her later at a masked ball, Chekhov promised to give her the answer to this from the stage in his new play. Ronald Hingley, in his biography of Chekhov, recounts how she went to the catastrophic first night in St. Petersburg and struggled to hear the promised answer through the uproar all around her. She noted the page-reference given by Nina to locate the passage in Trigorin's works, and when she got home looked up the same page and line in a volume of her own stories. It read: 'Young ladies should not attend masked balls.' By this time, anyway, says Hingley, Chekhov had passed Avilova's fervently inscribed charm on to Komissarzhevskaya, the actress playing Nina, and it was being used on stage as a prop. If Chekhov had modelled Trigorin's behaviour with women on his own the play would have been deprived of Acts Three and Four.

It has to be recognised, I think, that there are some elements in the play which Chekhov has not completely succeeded in accommodating to his new aesthetic. Arkadina's aside after she believes she has broken Trigorin's will to leave her, 'Now he's mine,' (at any rate if played 'to herself', as written) seems to stem more from nineteenth-century dramatic convention than from life. Still, she is an actress by profession; it may be she rather than Chekhov who has imported the line from the theatre. Then again, Konstantin's account in Act Four of what has happened to Nina over the past two years seems to me awkwardly and belatedly expository, dramatically inert, and curiously old-fashioned in tone. Again, though, a similar justification might be offered – that it is only natural for Konstantin, as a writer of the time, to talk like a nineteenth-century short story. The soliloquies, too, seem to me a breach of the convention that Chekhov has established. If we are elsewhere left, as we are in life, to work out for ourselves what people are thinking and feeling from what they actually choose or happen to say to each other, why should we suddenly be given direct access, by means of a traditional stage convention, to Dorn's actual thoughts about Konstantin's play, or to Konstantin's assessment of his own stories? I was tempted to reorganise the scenes a little to avoid the need for soliloquy (it could be done fairly easily). It is true that Chekhov was still relying on soliloquy in *Uncle Vanya*, but by the time he came to write the last two plays he had abandoned it. The only apparent exception is Firs, locked into the house alone at the end of *The Cherry Orchard*. But he is not really soliloquising; he is an old man talking to himself, as he has earlier even in other people's presence.

These are small points. The other complaints which are sometimes made against the play seem to me to stem from misunderstandings. The symbolism, for instance, is occasionally disparaged as a portentous device to be outgrown by Chekhov in the three later and even greater plays. There is in fact only one piece of symbolism – though it recurs throughout the play – and that is the motif of the seagull itself. Now for a start it is not true that symbolic images of this sort do not occur in the last three plays. Moscow plainly stands for much more than its geographical self in *Three Sisters*; so does Natasha's colonisation of the Prozorovs' house; while the cherry orchard and its destruction must be one of the most suggestive and powerful symbols ever used on the stage. In the second place the symbolism of the dead seagull is set up not by Chekhov but by Konstantin, as Nina immediately recognises when he lays the bird accusingly at her feet. It is part of the portentousness and inertness of Konstantin's art, not of Chekhov's – and it is then taken up by Trigorin and absorbed into the machinery of *his*, when he discovers the dead bird and outlines his story of the girl who is destroyed with the same wilfulness and casualness. Between them they burden Nina with an image for herself and her fate that comes to obsess her. One of the themes of the play, as I have argued, is the way in which art warps and destroys the life that it draws upon. The message of the seagull, as it stands there stuffed and forgotten at the end of the play, is precisely of the deadness of the symbolic process.

Many people, too, have had difficulty in the past with the scene in the last act between Nina and Konstantin. The difficulty has arisen because it has often been regarded, and played, as a version of the traditional mad scene, where the pathos of the heroine who has lost or been rejected by her love is demonstrated by her retreat from reality into a world of illusion. This is plainly not the case with Nina for the greater part of the scene; she gives an entirely clear, calm, and sane account of her experiences. The problem comes when she says, as she does in all the English translations of the play that I have come across, 'I am a seagull'. The poor girl thinks she is a bird; her mind in plainly going. Now, there is a much more reasonable construction to place upon her words here – and if there is a choice then a reasonable construction must surely always be preferred in interpreting a character's behaviour – but it is obscured by a difficulty in the translation of the Russian that may at first sight seem quibbingly small. In the Russian language there is no such thing as an article, either definite or indefinite. No distinction can be made, in speech or thought, between what English-speakers are forced to regard as two separable concepts – 'a seagull' and 'the seagull'. So when Nina signs her letters *'Chaika'* (Seagull), it is perfectly open to Konstantin to regard this as a sign of distraction, of the sort suffered by the grief-stricken miller in Pushkin's *Rusalka*, who tells people he is a raven. But what Nina herself means, surely, when the distinction has to be made in English, is not that she is *a* seagull but that she is *the* seagull. In other words, she is not identifying with the bird but with the girl in Trigorin's story, who is the Seagull in the same way that Jenny Lind was the Swedish Nightingale, or Shakespeare was the Swan of Avon. This is the idea that has seized hold of her – not that she has white wings and a yellow beak – but that she has been reduced to the status of a manipulated character in Trigorin's fiction – a character whose fate can be summed up in a single image. This is an obsessive thought, and she makes repeated efforts to throw it off, but it is not in any sense a deluded one. She *has* been manipulated; she is another victim of the distorting and deadening process of art. One can't help wondering if Avilova and Lika Mizinova ever came to feel that they had this in common with Nina, as well as everything else.

If her picture of herself as being the seagull of Trigorin's projected story is sane and sober, so is her claim to have found her way at last as an actress. We have no way of judging whether her hopes are well-founded; but her feeling that she is on the right path at last is an entirely rational one. Konstantin takes it seriously, anyway – seriously enough to realise that he by comparison is still lost, and to shoot himself in despair as a result. Faced with that testimony to the seriousness of his judgment we are scarcely in a position to dissent.

And this in fact is the final irony of the play – that in the end the Seagull herself escapes, wounded but still flying. It is the shooter who is shot, the writer who is written to death. Konstantin, not Nina, turns out to be the real victim of Trigorin's story, the true Seagull; Konstantin, who first brought the creature down to earth and declared it to be a symbol, is the one who ends up symbolised, lying as inert and irrelevant in the next room as the poor stuffed bird is in this. Perhaps Mizinova and the others found some symbolic comfort in that.

MICHAEL FRAYN

A Note on the Translation

I have been more ruthless than ever with the names. In English translation, it seems to me, the characters all become native English-speakers, and native English-speakers do not attempt foreign words and names. They are particularly unlikely to start on the treacherous combination of given-name-plus-patronymic that occurs so often in Russian, and would indeed be ill-advised to try, except perhaps in extreme circumstances, such as attempting to get a table in a Moscow restaurant by claiming acquaintance with the head waiter. Few of the occasions in the play when names are used in the Russian have survived this stringent test.

There are a number of literary allusions in the play, most of them, fortunately from a translator's point of view, to Shakespeare, and clearly identified as such by the characters who make them. But there are one or two others that should be mentioned. Sorin, in Act Three, goes into town to get away for a little from what he calls, in the original, 'this gudgeon's life'. I have slightly reorganised this to make it at any rate clear to non-anglers that gudgeons live in the mud on the river-bottom. But I can find no way to suggest the literary background of the allusion, which is to the fish in Saltykov-Shchedrin's chilling fable *The Wise Gudgeon*. Saltykov's gudgeon, terrified of being eaten by a pike or crushed by a crab, digs a hole in the mud and hides himself in it, only to emerge to snatch his food when everything else is asleep and then to rush back in terror, unable ever to fulfil his natural function in life by marrying and having children. 'And in this way', says Saltykov, 'the wise gudgeon lived a hundred years and more. And all the time he trembled and he trembled. Neither friends nor relations did he have; he neither went to see anyone nor did anyone come to see him. He never played cards, nor drank strong drink, nor smoked tobacco, nor chased after pretty girls – only trembled and thought the one same thought: "God be praised, I seem to be alive!"' This is the picture of Sorin's life that the original would suggest to a Russian audience. The danger that terrifies the poor gudgeon most, incidentally, is the prospect of being caught by an angler and turned into fish-soup – a fate which Sorin avoided but which one might think Nina did not.

Konstantin, in Act Four, refers to the mad miller in *Rusalka*. This is the fragment of a verse-drama by Pushkin about a miller's daughter who is made pregnant and abandoned by a prince. She throws herself into the millstream, whereupon her father becomes demented with grief, and declares that he is the raven of the locality. The drowned girl herself becomes a *rusalka*, a water-spirit like a mermaid, and seems to be on the point of getting her revenge when the fragment ends. The parallel with Nina and Trigorin is obvious.

There is another quotation, or what appears to be a quotation, that I have not been able to identify. Arkadina's line in Act One, given here as 'Come, then, away, ill-starred old man', appears in Russian to be metrical in form and poetic in vocabulary and word-order. I assume it is a line from some part which Arkadina has played, and indeed in an earlier draft of the act she goes on to add: 'In some play or other it says: "Come to your senses, old man!"' Arkadina's line in Act Two, given here as 'I am troubled in my soul', also looks suspiciously poetic in the original. I have consulted a number of sources and a number of Russian friends without success. The lines may well be from forgotten plays, or even entirely fictitious. On the other hand there may be a little more meaning to be gleaned here.

Chekhov gives precise references for all the songs that Sorin and Dorn sing to themselves. I have retained the titles of only the two which may still be familiar. The others, which have disappeared into the mists of time and would be entirely unfamiliar even if disinterred from the archives, I have reduced to unspecified humming. On the other hand I have slightly expanded Dorn's reference to Jupiter's anger in Act One to reconstruct the classical saying to which it alludes.

I have followed the new and authoritative 30-volume *Complete Collected Works and Letters* in restoring the cuts and changes demanded by the censor. Potapenko, the friend who was ironically (see Introduction) charged with shepherding the text through the process of censorship, reported to Chekhov that there were unexpected difficulties. 'Your Decadent looks with indifference upon his mother's love affairs, which is not allowed by the censor's rules.' The censor himself later wrote to Chekhov direct to remove all doubt about what he wanted done. 'I have marked a number of places in blue pencil', he explained, 'in addition to which I think I should make clear that I had in mind not so much the expressions themselves as the general sense of the relations established by these expressions. The point is not the cohabitation of the actress and the writer, but the calm view taken of this state of affairs by her son and her brother.' Negotiations dragged on throughout the summer of 1896, with Chekhov making some changes and Potapenko making others. After one suggested alteration, in a letter to Potapenko, Chekhov added in exasperation: 'Or whatever you like, even a text from the Talmud.' In the first printed text of the play, in journal form in December 1896, which was not subject to theatrical censorship, Chekhov reverted to his original text. It is true that in all the subsequent book editions he used the censored text; but these were published with the assurance on the title-page that the plays they contained had been 'passed unconditionally by the censorship for production'. The changes are small and of no very great significance, but there seems no possible reason now for not using the text that Chekhov himself plainly wanted.

There is a double irony, as things turned out, in Konstantin's allusion to the censorship in the first act – one intended by Konstantin and another added by circumstance. I have slightly expanded the reference, to make it comprehensible while leaving it oblique (Russian audiences, of course, have more experience in reading between the lines). Konstantin explains his premature departure from university by likening himself to an item which has failed to appear in the press 'owing to circumstances beyond the editor's control'. Chekhov had the same difficulty with Trofimov in *The Cherry Orchard* – how to explain that someone had been expelled from university for his political activities. It was impossible to get a direct reference to this past the censor – but not, apparently, a reference to the process of censorship itself.

M.F.

Characters

ARKADINA, *an actress*
KONSTANTIN, *her son*
SORIN, *her brother*
NINA, *the young daughter of a wealthy landowner*
SHAMRAYEV, *a retired lieutenant, Sorin's steward*
POLINA, *his wife*
MASHA, *his daughter*
TRIGORIN, *a novelist*
DORN, *a doctor*
MEDVEDENKO, *a teacher*
YAKOV, *a workman*
A MAN COOK
A MAID

The action takes place on Sorin's country estate.
Between Acts Three and Four two years have elapsed.

The Pronunciation of the Names

The following is an approximate practical guide. In general, all stressed a's are pronounced as in 'far' (the sound is indicated below by 'aa') and all stressed o's as in 'more' (they are written below as 'aw'). All unstressed a's and o's are thrown away and slurred. The u's are pronounced as in 'crude'; they are shown below as 'oo'. A y at the beginning of a syllable, in front of another vowel, is pronounced as a consonant (i.e. as in 'yellow', not as in 'sky').

The characters:

Aar*kaar*deena (I*reen*a)
Konstan*teen* (*Kawst*ya)
*Sawr*een (Pe*troosh*a)
*Neen*a
Sham-*rye*-yev
Po*leen*a
*Maash*a
Tri*gawr*een (Bo*rees* Alek*say*eveech)
Dawrn (Yev*gay*ni)
Medved*yenk*o (Sem*yawn*)
*Yaak*ov

Other names occurring in the play, in alphabetical order:

Chadin, Pashka – *Chaad*een, *Paash*ka
Gogol – *Gawg*ol
Grokholsky – Gro*khawl*sky
Izmailov – Iz-*my*-lov
Kharkov – *Khaar*kov

Krechinsky – Kre*chee*nsky
Mama – *Maam*a
Matryona – Matr*yawn*a
Molchanovka – Mol*chaan*ovka
Nekrasov – Ne*kraass*ov
Odessa – O*dyess*a
Papa – *Paap*a
Poltava – Pol*taav*a
Sadovsky – Sa*dawv*sky
Silva – *Seel*va
Slavyansky Bazar – Sla*vy*ansky Ba*zaar*
Suzdaltzev – *Sooz*daltzev
Tolstoy – Tol*stoy*
Turgenyev – T*oor-gain*-yev
Yeletz – Ye*letz*
Yevgeni – Yev*gain*i

Act One

Birds Chirping watersounds

✻ Pre Recorded

crickets echoing off the waves of the lake,

A section of the park on SORIN's *estate. A broad avenue leads away from the audience into the depths of the park towards the lake. The avenue is closed off by a stage which has been hurriedly run up for some home entertainment, so that the lake is completely invisible. Right and left of the stage is a shrubbery. A few chairs and a garden table.*

The sun has just set. On the improvised stage, behind the lowered curtain, are YAKOV *and other* WORKMEN; *coughing and banging can be heard.* MASHA *and* MEDVEDENKO *enter left, on their way back from a walk.*

MEDVEDENKO. Why do you always wear black?

MASHA. I'm in mourning for my life. I'm unhappy.

MEDVEDENKO. Why? (*Reflectively.*) I don't understand. You've got your health. Your father may not be rich, but he's not badly off. I have a much harder time than you. I get 23 rubles a month all told – less deductions for the pension – and I don't go round in mourning.

They sit.

MASHA. It's not a question of money. Even a beggar can be happy.

MEDVEDENKO. Theoretically. In practice it comes down to this: my mother and I, plus my two sisters and my little brother – and only 23 rubles a month coming in. You mean we don't have to eat and drink? There's no need for tea and sugar? No need for tobacco? I don't know how to manage.

MASHA (*looking round at the improvised stage*). The show will be starting soon.

MEDVEDENKO. Yes. A play written by Konstantin, and his

Nina will be acting in it. Two people in love, and today their souls will merge as they strive to create a single artistic impression. Whereas my soul and yours have no point of contact. I love you – I can't stay at home I long to see you so much – I walk three miles here and three miles back every day – and all I get from you is indifference. Well, it's understandable. I've no money – I've a large family . . . Who wants to marry a man who can't even support himself?

MASHA. Oh, fiddle. (*Takes a pinch of snuff.*) I'm very touched that you love me, but I can't say the same in return, and that's all there is to it. (*Offers him the snuffbox.*) Have a pinch.

MEDVEDENKO. Not for me.

Pause.

MASHA. So close. We'll probably have a storm during the night. If you're not philosophising you're going on about money. You seem to think the worst thing that can happen to anyone is poverty, but I think it's a thousand times easier to go round in rags and beg your bread than it is to . . . Well, you wouldn't understand . . .

Enter, right, SORIN *and* KONSTANTIN.

SORIN (*leaning on a stick*). The thing with me, though, is that I somehow never feel quite up to the mark when I'm in the country. No question about it – I'll never get used to being here. Went to bed at ten last night and woke up at nine this morning feeling I'd slept for so long that my brain had stuck to my skull, etcetera, etcetera. (*Laughs.*) Then after dinner I dropped off again, and now I feel as if a horse and cart had gone over me. It's like being in a bad dream, when all's said and done . . .

KONSTANTIN. You're right – you ought to be living in town. (*Sees* MASHA *and* MEDVEDENKO.) Listen, you'll be called when it starts – you're not supposed to be here now. Go away, will you.

SORIN (*to* MASHA). And would you mind asking your father to have the dog let loose? It howls otherwise. My sister was awake all night again.

MASHA. You can talk to my father yourself – I'm not going to. Spare me that, at any rate. (*To* MEDVEDENKO.) Come on, then.

MEDVEDENKO (*to* KONSTANTIN). You'll let us know before it starts, then.

Exeunt MASHA *and* MEDVEDENKO.

SORIN. So the dog will be howling all night again. It's a funny thing – I've never been able to live as I please when I've been in the country. In the old days I used to take a month's leave and come here to relax, simple as that, but then they'd so pester you with all kinds of nonsense that from the moment you arrived you'd want to be away again . . . Now I'm retired, though, there's nowhere else to go, when all's said and done. Like it or lump it . . .

YAKOV (*to* KONSTANTIN). We're off for a swim, then.

KONSTANTIN. All right, but I want you standing by in ten minutes time. (*Looks at his watch.*) Not long before it starts.

YAKOV. Sir.

Exit YAKOV.

KONSTANTIN (*glancing over the improvised stage*). Now how about this for a theatre. Curtain at the front, wings at the side – then nothing beyond but empty space. No scenery. The back of the stage opening straight on to the lake and the horizon. The curtain goes up at half-past eight precisely, as the moon rises.

SORIN. Splendid.

KONSTANTIN. If Nina's late then of course the whole effect will be ruined. She ought to be here by now. Her father and stepmother keep guard over her – getting out of the house is *raking sound as combs hair*

like escaping from prison. (*Adjusts his uncle's tie.*) Your hair
needs a comb through it – so does your beard. You could do
with a trim, couldn't you?

SORIN (*combing his beard*). It's the tragedy of my life. Even as
a young man I always looked as though I'd been at the bottle,
simple as that. Women never liked me. (*Sitting down.*) Why
is my sister out of sorts?

KONSTANTIN. Why? Because she's bored. (*Sitting down beside
him.*) Because she's jealous. She's already set her mind against
me, and against having theatricals, and against my play, in
case her novelist takes a fancy to Nina. She doesn't know
anything about my play, but she already hates it.

SORIN (*laughs*). Oh, come, come . . .

KONSTANTIN. She's already vexed that in this one little theatre
it's Nina who will have the success, and not her. (*Looks at his
watch.*) A comic tale of human psychology, my mother.
Talented, unquestionably; intelligent, quite capable of being
moved by a book. Recite you the whole of Nekrasov by heart.
Ministers to the sick like an angel. But you try saying
something nice about Duse in her hearing! Oh dear me no!
She's the one who has to have the nice things said about her
and no one else, she's the one who has to be written about,
shouted about, admired for her extraordinary performance in
La Dame aux Camélias, or whatever; and because this drug
isn't available here in the country she gets bored and ill-
tempered, and all of us become her enemies – it's all our
fault. Then again she's superstitious – she's afraid of three
candles and the thirteenth of the month. She's mean with her
money. She's got seventy thousand rubles sitting in a bank
in Odessa – I know that for a fact. But ask her if you can
borrow some and she'll burst into tears.

SORIN. You've got it into your head that your mother doesn't
like your play, and you're working yourself up about it in
advance, simple as that. Calm down, now – your mother
worships you.

KONSTANTIN (*pulling the petals off a flower*). She loves me – she loves me not . . . She loves me – loves me not . . . Loves me – loves me not. (*Laughs.*) There you are – she doesn't love me. Well, of course she doesn't. She wants to live and love and dress in light colours, and there am I, twenty-five years old, perpetually reminding her that she's stopped being young. When I'm not there she's thirty-two – when I am she's forty-three; and that's why she hates me. Then again I don't acknowledge the theatre. She loves the theatre – she thinks she's serving humanity and the sacred cause of art, whereas in my view the modern theatre is an anthology of stereotypes and received ideas. When the curtain goes up, and there, in a room with three walls lit by artificial lighting because it's always evening, these great artists, these high priests in the temple of art, demonstrate how people eat and drink, how they love and walk about and wear their suits; when out of these banal scenes and trite words they attempt to extract a moral – some small and simple moral with a hundred household uses; when under a thousand different disguises they keep serving me up the same old thing, the same old thing, the same old thing – then I run and don't stop running, just as Maupassant ran from the sight of the Eiffel Tower, that weighed on his brain with its sheer vulgarity.

SORIN. We couldn't do without the theatre.

KONSTANTIN. What we need are new artistic forms. And if we don't get new forms it would be better if we had nothing at all. (*Looks at his watch.*) I love my mother, I love her deeply. But then she smokes, she drinks, she quite openly lives with that novelist, they're always bandying her name about in the papers – and I'm sick of it. Though sometimes what prompts me is just ordinary mortal egotism; I start to regret that my mother is a well-known actress, and I feel I should be happier if she were an ordinary woman. Uncle, what could be sillier or more hopeless than the position I've found myself in often enough: solid rows of celebrities sitting in her drawing-room, artists and writers, and me the only one among them who's a nobody, being put up with purely because I'm her son. Who am I? What am I? I left university half-way through owing to circumstances beyond the editor's control, as the phrase goes; I've no talents; I've no money; while according to my passport I'm a shopkeeper, a Kiev shopkeeper. My father *did* come from Kiev, of course – he *was* from the shopkeeping classes – although he was also a well-known actor. So that when all those artists and writers in her drawing-room would turn their gracious attention upon me I had the impression that with every glance they were measuring the depth of my nonentity. I could guess what they were thinking, and the humiliation of it hurt . . .

SORIN. Speaking of writers, tell me, what sort of fellow is this novelist of hers? Difficult to make him out. He never says anything.

KONSTANTIN. He's intelligent, straightforward, a person of somewhat – shall we say? – melancholy disposition. A very decent sort of man. He's still well short of forty, but he's already famous and thoroughly jaded . . . These days he drinks nothing but beer and has no time for young people. If we're talking about his work then it's – how can I put it? – well, it's charming, it's clever . . but . . if you've read Tolstoy or Zola then you won't want to read Trigorin.

SORIN. Yes, but take me, now – I've a soft spot for literary men. Once upon a time there were two things I passionately wanted in life: I wanted to marry and I wanted to become a literary man, and I never managed either. So there we are. Nice to be even a minor literary man, when all's said and done.

KONSTANTIN (*listens*). I can hear footsteps . . . (*Embraces his uncle.*) I can't live without her . . . Even the sound of her footsteps is wonderful . . . I'm so happy I don't know what I'm doing!

Goes quickly across to meet NINA *as she enters.*

My enchantress, my dream . . .

NINA (*anxiously*). I'm not late . . . Tell me I'm not late . . .

KONSTANTIN (*kissing her hands*). No, no, no . . .

NINA. I've been worrying about it all day. I was so terrified! I was afraid my father wouldn't let me go . . . But he's just gone out with my stepmother. The sky red – the moon already starting to rise – and I kept whipping and whipping the horse. (*Laughs.*) I'm glad, though. (*Firmly presses* SORIN's *hand.*)

SORIN (*laughs*). We've been crying, haven't we . . . We can't have that, now.

NINA. It's nothing . . . Look how out of breath I am. I'm going in half-an-hour, we must hurry. You mustn't, mustn't, for heaven's sake, make me late. My father doesn't know I'm here.

KONSTANTIN. It's time to start, in any case. We must go and call everyone.

SORIN. I'll do it. Right away, simple as that. (*Goes off right, singing Schumann's 'Two Grenadiers', then looks round.*) I started singing like that once, and one of the deputy prosecutors looked at me and said: 'You know, sir, you have a very powerful voice.' Then he thought for a moment and he added: 'Very powerful, but very disagreeable.' (*Laughs and goes off.*)

NINA. My father and his wife won't let me come here. They say you're all Bohemians . . . They're afraid I might run off to be an actress . . . But it's the lake that draws me here, like a seagull . . . My heart's full of you. (*Looks round.*)

KONSTANTIN. We're alone.

NINA. I think there's someone there . .

They kiss.

NINA. What sort of tree is that?

KONSTANTIN. Elm.

NINA. Why does it have such a dark colour?

KONSTANTIN. It's evening – everything looks dark. Don't go early, please don't.

NINA. I can't stay.

KONSTANTIN. Supposing I came to your house, Nina? I'll stand in the garden all night and look up at your window.

NINA. You can't – the watchman will see you. Treasure's not used to you yet – he'll bark.

KONSTANTIN. I love you.

NINA. Shh . . .

KONSTANTIN (*hearing footsteps*). Who's that? Is that you, Yakov?

YAKOV (*behind the improvised stage*). Sir.

KONSTANTIN. Stand by. Time to start. Is the moon rising?

YAKOV. Sir.

KONSTANTIN. Have you got the spirits? And the sulphur? When the red eyes appear there must be a smell of sulphur. (*To* NINA.) Go on, then, it's all ready. Are you nervous?

NINA. Yes, very. I don't mind your mother, I'm not afraid of her, but you've got Trigorin here . . . When I think of acting in front of him I'm terrified, I'm ashamed . . . He's a famous writer . . . Is he young?

KONSTANTIN. Yes, he is.

NINA. Such wonderful stories he writes!

KONSTANTIN (*coldly*). I wouldn't know. I haven't read them.

NINA. Your play's so difficult to do. It doesn't have any living characters.

KONSTANTIN. Living characters! The point is not to show life the way it is, or the way it ought to be, but the way it comes to you in dreams.

NINA. It doesn't have much action, your play – it's just a kind of reading. And I think a play absolutely has to have love in it . . .

They both go behind the improvised stage. Enter POLINA *and* DORN.

POLINA. It's getting damp. Go back and put your galoshes on.

DORN. I'm hot.

POLINA. You won't look after yourself. It's just pig-headedness. You're a doctor – you know perfectly well that dampness in the air is bad for you, but no, you want to make me suffer. Last night you sat out on the verandah all evening just to spite me . . .

> DORN *hums*.

You were so wrapped up in your conversation with *her* – you never noticed the cold. Admit it, now – you're fond of her.

DORN. I'm fifty-five.

POLINA. Oh, fiddle, that's not old for a man. You're perfectly well preserved and you're still attractive to women.

DORN. So what do you want me to do?

POLINA. You'll all bow down in front of an actress. Not one of you who won't!

DORN (*hums*). If artists are popular people, if they get treated differently from – what shall we say? – from businessmen, then that's the way the world's made. That's our yearning for higher things.

POLINA. You've always had women falling in love with you and hanging round your neck. Is that supposed to be a yearning for higher things?

DORN (*shrugs*). If you like. There's been much that was good in the relationships women have had with me. What they liked most about me was the fact I was a first-class doctor. Ten years or so back, you may recall, I was the only one in the whole province who could deliver a baby decently. Added to which I was always a man of honour.

POLINA (*seizes his hand*). Oh, my dear!

DORN. Hush, now. They're coming.

> *Enter* ARKADINA *on* SORIN's *arm*, TRIGORIN, SHAMRAYEV, MEDVEDENKO, *and* MASHA.

SHAMRAYEV. In 1873, at Poltava during the Fair, she gave an amazing performance. Sheer delight! A wonderful performance! And do you know where Chadin is these days, the comic actor? In *Krechinsky's Wedding* there was no one to touch him – he was better than Sadovsky, I promise you, dear lady. Where is he these days?

ARKADINA. You keep asking me about people who came out of the Ark! How should I know? (*Sits.*)

SHAMRAYEV (*sighs*). Pashka Chadin! They don't make them like that any more. The theatre's not what it was. Once there were mighty oaks – now we see mere stumps.

DORN. There's not much in the way of brilliant talent these days, it's true, but your average actor is of a much higher standard.

SHAMRAYEV. I can't agree. Though it's all a question of taste. *De gustibus aut bene aut nihil.*

KONSTANTIN *comes out from behind the improvised stage.*

ARKADINA (*to* KONSTANTIN). But, my precious, when's it going to begin?

KONSTANTIN. In a minute. If you would just be patient.

ARKADINA. 'O Hamlet, speak no more:
Thou turn'st mine eyes into my very soul;
And there I see such black and grained spots
As will not leave their tinct.'

KONSTANTIN. 'Nay, but to live
In the rank sweat of an enseamed bed
Stew'd in corruption, honeying and making love
Over the nasty sty . . .'

A horn sounds behind the improvised stage.

Ladies and gentlemen, the performance is about to begin. Your attention, if you please. (*Pause.*) I'm going to start. (*Knocks with a stick and speaks in a loud voice.*) You honoured ancient shades that hover in the hours of night above this lake, make our eyes grow heavy, and let us dream of what will be in two hundred thousand years from now!

SORIN. In two hundred thousand years from now there won't be anything.

KONSTANTIN. Then let them show us this not-anything.

ARKADINA. Let them. We're fast asleep.

The curtain rises. The view over the lake is revealed, with the moon above the horizon and its reflection in the water. On a large stone sits NINA, all in white.

NINA. Men and lions, partridges and eagles, spiders, geese, and antlered stags, the unforthcoming fish that dwelt beneath the waters, starfish and creatures invisible to the naked eye; in short – all life, all life, all life, its dismal round concluded, has guttered out . . . Thousands of centuries have passed since any living creature walked the earth, and this poor moon in vain lights up her lantern. In the meadows the dawn cry of the crane is heard no more, and the May bugs are silent in the lime groves. Cold, cold, cold. Empty, empty, empty. Fearful, fearful, fearful. (*Pause.*) The bodies of all living creatures have fallen into dust, and Everlasting Matter has turned them into stones, into water, into clouds; while all their souls have merged into one. And this one universal world soul is me . . . me . . . In me are the souls of Alexander the Great, of Caesar, of Shakespeare, of Napoleon, and of the least of leeches. In me the consciousness of human beings has merged with the instincts of animals. All, all, all do I remember, and every life I live again in my own self.

Marsh-lights appear.

ARKADINA (*quietly*). A touch of the Decadent School here, I think.

KONSTANTIN (*pleading and reproachful*). Mama!

NINA. I am quite alone. Once in every hundred years I open my lips to speak, and my voice echoes cheerlessly through this emptiness where no one listens . . . Even you, pale fires, are not listening to me . . . In the late watches of the night you are born from the rotting swamp, and wander the world till dawn, yet without the power of thought or will, without a flicker of life. For fear that life might appear to you, the Father of Eternal Matter, who is the Devil, effects in you, as he does in stones and water, a constant replacement of the atoms, and you are in a state of continual flux. One thing alone in the universe stays unchanging and constant – spirit itself. (*Pause.*) Like a prisoner flung into some deep dry well I have no knowledge of where I am or of what awaits me. All I am allowed to know is that in this stubborn, bitter struggle with the Devil, marshal of all material forces, I am fated to be victor; and that matter and spirit will thereafter merge in wondrous harmony to usher in the reign of Universal Will. But that will come about only after long tens of thousands of years, when moon and bright Sirius and earth alike will gradually turn to dust . . .

Pause. Two red spots appear against the background of the lake.

Here comes my mighty adversary, the Devil, now. I see his fearful crimson eyes . . .

ARKADINA. There's a smell of sulphur. Is there supposed to be?

KONSTANTIN. Yes.

ARKADINA (*laughs*). I see – it's an effect.

KONSTANTIN. Mama!

NINA. He pines for human company . . .

POLINA (*to* DORN). You've taken your hat off. Put it on – you'll catch cold.

ARKADINA. He's taken it off to the Devil, the Father of Eternal Matter.

KONSTANTIN (*out loud, losing his temper*). Right, the play's over! That's it! Curtain!

ARKADINA. What are you getting cross about?

KONSTANTIN. That's it! Curtain! Can we have the curtain, please? (*Stamps his foot.*) Curtain!

The curtain is lowered.

I'm sorry! I was forgetting that playwriting and acting are reserved for the chosen few. I've infringed their monopoly! It . . . I . . .

He tries to say something else, but then flaps his hand and goes off left.

ARKADINA. What's got into him?

SORIN. Irina, my dear girl, that really is no way to deal with youthful pride.

ARKADINA. Why, what did I say?

SORIN. You offended him.

ARKADINA. He told us himself beforehand – it was an amusing skit. That's how I took it – as a skit.

SORIN. All the same . . .

ARKADINA. Now it turns out to be some great work of art! Oh, for heaven's sake! So he got up all this performance and perfumed the air with sulphur not to amuse us but to give us all an object-lesson in the art of writing and acting. Really, it's becoming a bore. These perpetual attacks on me, this campaign of pinpricks – it would tax the patience of a saint! He's a wilful, difficult boy.

SORIN. He wanted to give you pleasure.

ARKADINA. Oh, really? But he didn't pick some normal kind of play to do it with, did he? – He made us sit through these weary poetic ravings. For the sake of amusement I'm prepared to sit through even the ravings of delirium, but what we had here, I take it, were pretensions to new theatrical forms, to a new artistic era. So far as I could see, though, we didn't get new forms, we simply got bad manners.

TRIGORIN. Each of us writes as his fancy takes him and his talent allows.

ARKADINA. Let him write as his fancy takes him and his talent allows, just so long as he leaves me alone.

DORN. Jupiter wroth means Jupiter wrong.

ARKADINA. I'm not Jupiter – I'm a woman. (*Lights a cigarette.*) I'm not angry – I merely find it a bore that a young man should spend his time in such a tedious way. I didn't mean to offend him.

MEDVEDENKO. No one has any basis for separating spirit from matter, because for all we know spirit is nothing but the totality of material atoms. (*To* TRIGORIN, *with animation.*) But, you know, what someone ought to put in a play is how we teachers live. A hard, hard time we have of it!

ARKADINA. I'm sure you do, but let's not talk about either plays or atoms. Such a glorious evening! Listen, everyone – is that singing? (*Listens.*) How lovely!

POLINA. It's on the other side of the lake.

Pause.

ARKADINA (*to* TRIGORIN). Sit beside me. Ten years or so back on the lake here you could hear constant music and singing almost every night. There were six estates on this side. I remember laughter and noise and guns going off and everyone falling in love, falling in love . . . And the leading actor in all of this, the idol of all six estates, was . . . here he is – (*She nods at* DORN.) – the doctor. He's enchanting even now, but in those days he was irresistible. My conscience is beginning to prick, however. Why did I offend that poor boy of mine? I feel uneasy. (*Calls.*) Kostya! My son! Kostya!

MASHA. I'll go and look for him.

ARKADINA. Would you, my dear?

MASHA (*moving off left*). Halloo-oo! Halloo-oo!

She goes off. NINA *comes out from behind the improvised stage.*

NINA. We're obviously not going to do any more of it – I might as well come out. Hello.

She exchanges kisses with ARKADINA *and* POLINA.

SORIN. Bravo! Bravo!

ARKADINA. Bravo! Bravo! We all thought you were wonderful. With those looks, with that marvellous voice, you simply cannot stay lost in the depths of the countryside – it would be a sin. I'm sure you must have a talent. You hear? You absolutely must go on the stage!

NINA. Oh, that's my dream! (*Sighs.*) It will never come true, though.

ARKADINA. Who knows? Now, may I introduce: Trigorin – Boris Alekseyevich.

NINA. Oh, I'm so pleased to meet you . . . (*Overcome with embarrassment.*) I read everything you write . . .

ARKADINA (*sitting* NINA *down beside her*). Don't be embarrassed, my dear. He's a famous man, but he has a simple heart. You see – he's as embarrassed as you are.

DORN. I suggest they take the curtain up now. It's eerie like that.

SHAMRAYEV (*calls*). Yakov, take the curtain up, there's a good fellow!

The curtain goes up.

NINA (*to* TRIGORIN). It's a strange play, didn't you think?

TRIGORIN. I couldn't understand a word of it. I enjoyed watching it, though. You did it with such sincerity. And the scenery was lovely. (*Pause.*) There must be a lot of fish in that lake.

NINA. Yes, there are.

TRIGORIN. I love fishing. There's no greater pleasure I know than sitting on the bank at the end of the day and watching the float.

NINA. But I think that for anyone who has experienced the

pleasure of creating something all other pleasures must pale into insignificance.

ARKADINA (*laughing*). You mustn't talk like that. When people say nice things to him he just wishes the earth would swallow him up.

SHAMRAYEV. I remember an occasion at the Opera in Moscow when Silva, the famous bass, sang bottom C. Now that night, with malice aforethought, the bass from our church choir was sitting up in the gallery. Imagine our utter astonishment when suddenly we hear from the gallery, 'Bravo, Silva!' – a whole octave lower . . . Like this. (*In a deep but insubstantial bass.*) 'Bravo, Silva!' The whole theatre simply froze.

Pause.

DORN. A quiet angel flew past.

NINA. I must go. Goodbye.

ARKADINA. Go where? So early? We shan't let you.

NINA. Papa's waiting for me.

ARKADINA. Cruel man! Really . . .

They kiss.

Well, if you must you must. Such a shame to let you go.

NINA. If you knew how hard it is for me to leave!

ARKADINA. Someone ought to see you home, my pet.

NINA (*in alarm*). Oh, no, no!

SORIN (*pleading with her*). Do stay!

NINA. I really can't.

SORIN. Stay for one hour, simple as that. No harm, surely.

NINA (*on the verge of tears, after she has thought for a moment*). I mustn't! (*Presses his hand and quickly goes off.*)

ARKADINA. An unlucky girl, if truth be told. Apparently her late mother made all her huge wealth over to her husband – every last kopeck. Now the girl is left with nothing because her father in his turn has already made the whole lot over to his second wife. It's quite scandalous.

DORN. A real swine, though, her father, to give him his due.

SORIN (*rubbing his chilled hands*). We'd better be going, too, or it will get damp. My legs are aching.

ARKADINA. You look as if you've got a pair of wooden legs – you can scarcely walk on them. Come, then, away, ill-starred old man.

She takes his arm.

SHAMRAYEV (*offering* POLINA *his arm*). Madame?

SORIN. I can hear that dog howling again. (*To* SHAMRAYEV.) Be a good fellow, would you, and tell them to let it loose?

SHAMRAYEV. Can't be let loose, I regret to say. I'm afraid of thieves getting into the granary. I've got the millet in there. (*To* MEDVEDENKO, *who is walking beside him.*) Yes, a whole octave lower – 'Bravo, Silva!' And he wasn't an opera singer – just a simple member of the church choir.

MEDVEDENKO. What would someone in a church choir be paid?

Everyone except DORN *goes off.*

DORN (*alone*). Well, I don't know, I may be stupid, I may be mad, but I liked the play. There's something in it. When that little girl was talking about being on her own – and then when the Devil's red eyes appeared – I could feel my hands shaking with excitement. Something fresh and untutored about it . . . Here he comes, I think. I'd like to be a little nicer to him.

Enter KONSTANTIN.

KONSTANTIN. They've all gone.

DORN. I'm here.

KONSTANTIN. Masha's been looking all over the park for me. Intolerable woman.

DORN. Listen, I liked your play very much indeed. It was a strange kind of thing, and I didn't see the end of it, but it made a powerful impression none the less. You have talent; you must go on.

> KONSTANTIN *squeezes his hand hard and embraces him impetuously.*

So over-sensitive! Tears in your eyes . . . What was I going to say? Yes, you took a subject from the realm of abstract ideas. That was right, because a work of art must always express some substantial thought. Nothing can be excellent unless it be serious. You look quite pale!

KONSTANTIN. So you're saying – 'Go on'!

DORN. I am . . . But write about nothing that isn't important and eternal. I've lived my life with variety and taste, I'm a contented man, but I can tell you, if it had been granted to me to experience the lift of the heart that artists know in the moment of creation, then I think I should have scorned this material envelope of mine, and everything to do with it, and I should have left the ground and soared up into the heights.

KONSTANTIN. I'm sorry – where's Nina?

DORN. And another thing. In anything you write there must be a clear and definite thought. You must know why you're writing. If you don't, if you go down the picturesque path that has no definite goal at the end of it, then you'll lose your way, and your talent will destroy you.

KONSTANTIN (*impatiently*). Where's Nina?

DORN. She went home.

KONSTANTIN (*in despair*). What am I going to do? I want to see her . . . I have to see her . . . I'm going to go there . . .

> *Enter* MASHA.

DORN (*to* KONSTANTIN). Now, calm down, my friend.

KONSTANTIN. I'm going to go, all the same. I must go.

MASHA (*to* KONSTANTIN). Will you go into the house? Your mother's waiting. She's feeling uneasy about you.

KONSTANTIN. Tell her I've gone. And please, all of you, leave me alone! Just leave me alone! Don't follow me around!

DORN. Now, now, now, come on . . . Not the way . . . Not right.

KONSTANTIN (*on the verge of tears*). Goodbye, doctor. Thank you . . .

He goes off.

DORN (*sighs*). Youth, youth!

MASHA. Whenever there's nothing more to be said then people say: 'Youth, youth . . .' (*Takes a pinch of snuff.*)

DORN (*takes the snuffbox away from her and flings it into the bushes*). That's a filthy habit! (*Pause.*) I think they've started playing cards inside. I must go.

MASHA. Wait a moment.

DORN. What is it?

MASHA. Yet another thing I want to tell you. I'd like to talk for a moment . . . (*Becoming agitated.*) I don't like my father . . . but you have a special place in my heart. I don't know why, but all my life I've felt you were close to me . . . Help me. Please help me, or I shall do something silly – I shall make a mockery of my life, I shall ruin it . . . I can't go on . . .

DORN. What do you mean? Help you with what?

MASHA. I'm in such torment. No one knows, no one knows the torment I'm in! (*Lays her head on his breast; quietly.*) I'm in love with Konstantin.

DORN. You're all so over-sensitive! So over-sensitive! And so much love around . . . Oh, the spells woven by this lake! (*Tenderly.*) But what can I do, my child? What can I do?

CURTAIN

Act Two

The croquet lawn. In the distance to the right is the house, with a wide verandah, while to the left can be seen the lake, with the sun sparkling on it. Flower-beds and midday heat. At the side of the lawn, on a garden seat in the shade of an old lime-tree, are sitting ARKADINA, DORN, *and* MASHA. DORN *has a book open in his lap.*

ARKADINA (*to* MASHA). Both of us stand up.

> *They both stand.*

Side by side. Now, you're twenty-two and I'm nearly twice that. Doctor, which of us is the younger-looking?

DORN. You are, of course.

ARKADINA. You see? And why? Because I work, I'm alive to the world around me, I'm always busy; whereas you're such a stick-in-the-mud, you don't know how to live . . . Also I make it a rule not to look into the future. I never think about old age, I never think about death. What will be, will be.

MASHA. Yes, but I feel as though I'd been born a long, long time ago; I'm dragging my life behind me like a dress with an endless train . . . And often I've no desire to go on living. (*Sits.*) Well, that's all nonsense, of course. You just have to shake yourself out of it.

> DORN *quietly sings Siebel's aria, 'Faites-lui mes aveux,' from Act III of Gounod's* Faust.

ARKADINA. Then again, my dear, I'm as careful about my appearance as an Englishman. I always keep myself firmly in hand. My dress, my hair – always *comme il faut*. Should I ever allow myself to go out of the house – even into the garden here – in a housecoat, or with my hair not done? Never. If I've kept my looks it's because I've never stopped caring about my appearance, I've never let myself go in the way that some women do . . . (*Walks about the lawn, hands on her hips.*) There you are, you see – spry as a kitten. I could play a girl of fifteen still.

DORN. Nonetheless and notwithstanding, I'm still reading, am I? (*Picks up the book.*) We stopped at the corn-chandler and the rats . . .

ARKADINA. And the rats, yes. Go on, then. (*Sits.*) Or rather, give it to me and I'll read. It's my turn. (*Takes the book and runs her eyes over it to find the place.*) The rats . . . Here we are . . . (*Reads.*) 'And, to be sure, it is as dangerous for people in society to make much of writers and to entice them into their homes as it would be for a corn-chandler to keep rats in his shop. And yet there is a vogue for them. So, when a woman has designs upon a writer whom she wishes to take up, she lays siege to him with compliments and attentions and little marks of favour . . . .' Well, that may be how it is with the French, but with us there's nothing like that – we don't work to a programme. Before a woman takes a writer up in this country she's usually head over heels in love with him, thank you very much. You don't have to look far – take me and Trigorin, for instance . . .

Enter SORIN, *leaning on his stick, with* NINA *beside him, and* MEDVEDENKO *pushing an empty wheelchair behind them.*

SORIN (*in the tone of voice used for being nice to a child*). So – we're all smiles, are we? We're all bright and cheerful today? (*To* ARKADINA.) We're all sunshine and smiles! Our father and stepmother have gone into town, and now we're as free as the air for three whole days.

NINA (*sits beside* ARKADINA *and embraces her*). I'm happy! I'm all yours now.

SORIN (*sits in his wheelchair*). As pretty as a picture she is today.

ARKADINA. Attractive, well turned out . . . What a sensible

girl. (*Kisses her.*) Still, we mustn't praise her too much or it will bring bad luck. Where's Trigorin?

NINA. He's at the bathing-place, fishing.

ARKADINA. You'd think he'd get bored with it. (*Resumes her book.*)

NINA. What are you reading?

ARKADINA. Maupassant, my sweet – *On the Water*. (*Reads a few lines to herself.*) Anyway, the next bit is neither amusing nor true. (*Shuts the book.*) I am troubled in my soul. Can anyone tell me what the matter is with my son? Why is he being so stern and boring? He spends whole days together on the lake – I scarcely see him.

MASHA. He's sick at heart. (*To* NINA, *shyly.*) Please – read a bit of his play!

NINA (*shrugs*). Do you really want me to? It's so dull!

MASHA (*restraining her enthusiasm*). When he reads something himself his eyes blaze and his face grows pale. He's got a wonderful sad voice; yes, and the manner of a poet.

SORIN *snores.*

DORN. Sleep well!

ARKADINA. Petrusha!

SORIN. Um?

ARKADINA. Are you asleep?

SORIN. Certainly not.

Pause.

ARKADINA. You're not having any medical attention, are you. It's not right.

SORIN. I'd be delighted to have some medical attention. It's the doctor here who won't give me any.

DORN. Medical attention? When you're sixty?

SORIN. Even when you're sixty you still want to live.

DORN (*irritably*). Tch! Well, take some valerian drops, then.

ARKADINA. I have a feeling it would be good for him to go to a spa somewhere.

DORN. All right. He could go to a spa. Or not go to a spa.

ARKADINA. Make sense of that, if you can!

DORN. There's nothing to make sense of. It's all perfectly plain.

Pause.

MEDVEDENKO. Your brother ought to give up smoking.

SORIN. Oh, fiddle.

DORN. No, not fiddle. Alcohol and tobacco make you lose the sense of yourself. Smoke a cigar or drink a glass of vodka and you're no longer you – you're you plus someone else. The self grows blurred, and you start to see yourself as a third person – not as 'I' but as 'he'.

SORIN (*laughs*). It's all very well for you to talk. You've lived in your time. But how about me? I spent twenty-eight years working in the Department of Justice, but I still haven't lived, when all's said and done, I still haven't experienced anything, and I long to live, no question about it. You've had your fill in life and you don't care any more, so you tend to be philosophical, but I want to live, and so I drink sherry at dinner and smoke cigars, it's as simple as that. As simple as that.

DORN. Life has to be taken seriously. Swallowing medicine when you're sixty and feeling sorry you didn't have much fun when you were young – forgive me if I'm blunt – but that's fatuous.

MASHA (*stands up*). It must be lunchtime. (*Walks limply and lethargically.*) My leg's gone to sleep . . . .

Exit MASHA.

DORN. Lunch . . . She's going to go and have a couple of drinks first.

SORIN. You can't expect a beggar to be happy.

DORN. Oh, pish, you old civil servant.

SORIN. You speak as someone who's had his fill in life.

ARKADINA. Oh, what could be more boring than this sweet
country boredom! Heat, quiet, nothing anyone wants to do,
everyone philosophising away . . . It's nice being with you,
my friends, it's a pleasure to listen to you, and yet . . . to be
sitting in a hotel room somewhere learning your lines – could
anything be better than that?

NINA (*enthusiastically*). Oh, yes! I know what you mean.

SORIN. It's better in town, no doubt about it. You sit in your
office, no one gets past the attendant without being
announced, there's the telephone, there are cabs in the street
– it's as simple as that . . .

> DORN *sings* '*Faites-lui mes aveux . . .*'

> *Enter* SHAMRAYEV, *followed by* POLINA.

SHAMRAYEV. So this is where they are! A very good day to you
all! (*Kisses* ARKADINA's *hand, then* NINA's.) Delighted to
find you in good health. (*To* ARKADINA.) My wife tells me
you're proposing to go into town together. Is this true?

ARKADINA. Yes, we are.

SHAMRAYEV. Hm . . . Well, splendid, splendid, but what are
you going *in*, dear lady? We're carting the rye today – all the
men are busy. And which horses were you thinking of using,
may I ask?

ARKADINA. Which horses? How should *I* know?

SORIN. We've got carriage horses, haven't we?

SHAMRAYEV (*becoming agitated*). The carriage horses? But
where am I going to get harness for them? Where am I going
to get harness? Amazing, isn't it? Past comprehension! Dear
lady! I revere your talent, I'll gladly give you ten years of my
life, but horses I cannot give you!

ARKADINA. But supposing I *have* to go? What an extraordinary
state of affairs!

SHAMRAYEV. Dear lady! You don't realise what farming
involves!

<!-- handwritten margin note: horses noises or stomping noise) -->

ARKADINA (*flares up*). Oh, the same old story! In that case, I'm leaving for Moscow today. Have horses rented for me in the village – otherwise I shall *walk* to the station!

SHAMRAYEV (*flares up*). In that case I resign! Find yourself another steward!

Exit SHAMRAYEV.

ARKADINA. Every summer here it's the same, every summer I'm insulted! I'm not going to set foot in this place again!

Exit ARKADINA *left, where the bathing-place is assumed to be. A minute later she can be seen crossing towards the house, followed by* TRIGORIN *with his fishing-rods and bucket.*

SORIN (*flares up*). This is downright impertinence! This is downright heaven knows what! I'm sick of it, when all's said and done. Fetch all the horses directly!

NINA (*to* POLINA). But saying no to someone like that, a famous actress! Surely her slightest wish – her slightest whim, even – is more important than your farming? It's simply unbelievable!

POLINA (*in despair*). What can I do? Put yourself in my position. What can I do?

SORIN (*to* NINA). Come on, we'll go to my sister. We'll all plead with her not to leave. Isn't that right? (*Looks in the direction that* SHAMRAYEV *went off.*) The intolerable man! The tyrant!

NINA (*stops him getting up*). Sit down, sit down . . . We'll push you there . . .

She and MEDVEDENKO *push the wheelchair.*

How terrible, though!

SORIN. Yes, yes, it *is* terrible . . . But he won't go – I'll have a talk with him by and by.

They go off. Only DORN *and* POLINA *remain.*

DORN. How boring people are. Really your husband ought to

be thrown out on his neck, but in fact the whole thing will
end with that old woman and his sister apologising to him.
You'll see!

POLINA. He's sent the carriage horses out to the fields with all
the others. Every day we have this sort of trouble. If you knew
how it upsets me! It's making me ill – look, I'm shaking . . .
He's so coarse – I can't bear it. (*Pleading.*) Yevgeni, my dear,
my precious, take me unto you . . . Time's running out for
us, we're not young any more, and oh, to stop hiding, even
at the end of our lives, to stop lying . . .

Pause.

DORN. I'm fifty-five. It's a little late in the day to change my
way of life.

POLINA. I know why you reject me – I know there are other
women besides me. You can't take them all unto you. I
understand that. Forgive me, I'm being tiresome.

NINA *appears near the house, picking flowers.*

DORN. No, no.

POLINA. I'm tormented by jealousy. Of course – you're a
doctor – you can't avoid women. I understand that . . .

NINA *approaches.*

DORN. What's going on in there?

NINA. She's crying, and her brother's got his asthma.

DORN (*gets up*). I'd better go and give them both some
drops . . .

NINA (*gives him the flowers*). Here, have these!

DORN. *Merci bien.* (*Goes towards the house.*)

POLINA (*going to him*). What lovely flowers! (*Near the house, in
muffled tones.*) Give me those flowers! Give me those flowers!

*As soon as she gets the flowers she tears them up and throws
them on the ground. They both go into the house.*

NINA (*alone*). How curious to see a famous actress crying, especially over such a tiny thing! And isn't this curious, too? – a famous writer, the darling of the public, someone they write about in all the papers, someone they sell pictures of, someone who's translated into foreign languages – and he spends the whole day fishing – he's delighted to have caught a couple of chub. I thought famous people were proud and unapproachable. I thought they despised the common herd – I thought their renown, the brilliance of their name, gave them a kind of revenge for the way the herd set birth and wealth above all else. But here they are crying, fishing, playing cards, laughing, and losing their tempers like everybody else . . .

Enter KONSTANTIN, *hatless, with a gun and a seagull he has killed.*

KONSTANTIN. You're alone?
NINA. Yes, I'm alone.

KONSTANTIN *lays the seagull at her feet.*

What does that signify?
KONSTANTIN. I had the dishonour to kill this seagull today. I'm laying it at your feet.
NINA. What's the matter with you? (*Picks the seagull up and looks at it.*)
KONSTANTIN (*after a pause*). Soon I shall kill myself in the same way.
NINA. You're not the person I used to know.
KONSTANTIN. No, I'm not. Not since you stopped being the person I used to know. You've changed towards me. You look at me coldly, you're embarrassed by my being here.
NINA. You've got so irritable recently. You put things obliquely all the time, in some kind of symbols. This seagull, too – this is obviously a symbol of something, but I'm sorry, I don't know what it means . . . (*Lays the seagull on the bench.*) I'm

too simple to understand you.

KONSTANTIN. It all started that evening when my play was such an idiotic failure. Women never forgive failure. I burnt it, every last torn-up shred of it. If you knew how unhappy I am! It's terrifying the way you've grown cold towards me – it's unbelievable – it's as if I'd woken up and found that this lake had dried up, or drained away into the earth. You just said that you were too simple to understand me. Oh, what is there to understand? The play wasn't liked, you despise my inspiration, you've begun to think of me as an ordinary person – a nonetity – someone like everybody else . . . (*Stamps his foot.*) I know just what you mean, just exactly what you mean! It's like having a nail in my brain, curse it – and curse this pride of mine, too, that sucks my blood, sucks it like a serpent . . .

Sees TRIGORIN, *who is reading a book as he walks.*

Here comes the man with the real talent, entering like Hamlet, even down to the book. (*Mimics him.*) 'Words, words, words . . .' The sun hasn't reached you yet, and already you're smiling, your expression has melted in its rays. I won't stand in your way.

He quickly goes off.

TRIGORIN (*noting something down in the book*). Takes snuff and drinks vodka . . . Always in black. Loved by teacher . . .

NINA. Hello.

TRIGORIN. Hello to you. An unexpected turn of events, I gather, means that we are leaving today. It's hardly probable that you and I will see each other again. A pity. I don't often get the chance to meet girls of your age, not ones who are also interesting and attractive, and I can't remember now – can't clearly picture to myself – what it feels like to be eighteen or nineteen. So the girls who appear in my stories usually strike a false note. I should have liked to put myself in your place

for a while, just for an hour or so, to find out how your mind
worked and what sort of creature you were.

NINA. I should have liked to put myself in your place for a
while.

TRIGORIN. Why?

NINA. To know what it felt like to be a famous and talented
writer. What *does* fame feel like? What is the sensation of
being famous?

TRIGORIN. What does it feel like? It doesn't feel like anything,
so far as I know. I've never thought about it. (*After a moment's
reflection*.) Either you have an exaggerated idea of how famous
I am, or else it has no sensation at all.

NINA. But when you read about yourself in the papers?

TRIGORIN. If they're praising me it's nice. If they're abusing
me then I feel put out for a couple of days.

NINA. Strange and marvellous world! If you knew how I envied
you! People have such different lots in life. Some of them can
scarcely drag out their dull, obscure existence – all of them
alike, all of them unhappy; while others – you, for example
– you're one in a million – you're granted an absorbing, sunlit
life that's full of meaning . . . You're happy . . .

TRIGORIN. Me? (*Shrugs*.) Hm . . . You talk about fame and
happiness and some kind of absorbing, sunlit life, but to me
– forgive me – all these fine words are like those soft, sticky
sweets – the sort I never eat. You're very young and you're
very kind.

NINA. You have a wonderful life!

TRIGORIN. What's so specially good about it, though? (*Looks
at his watch*.) I have to go and write. I'm sorry, I'm rather
pressed for time . . . (*Laughs*.) You've trodden on my pet
corn, as they say, and I'm starting to get worked up and
slightly irritated. All right, then – let's talk about it. Let's talk
about my wonderful sunlit life . . . Now, where shall we
begin? (*After a moment's thought*.) There are things in this
world called *idées fixes*, when day and night a man can think

of nothing else except the moon, let's say. I have such a moon of my own. Day and night I am in the grip of a single obsession: I have to write, I have to write, I have to write . . . Scarcely have I finished one story than for some reason I have to write another, and then a third, and after the third a fourth . . . I write without cease, like a traveller with a fresh relay of horses waiting at every post, and I can't do otherwise. I ask you – what's sunlit or wonderful about that? It's a cruel life! Here I am talking to you, getting myself quite worked up, but at the same time I don't forget for a single moment that I have an unfinished story waiting for me. I see that cloud up there, looking like a grand piano, and I think, I shall have to put in a story somewhere that there was a cloud in the sky looking like a grand piano. I smell the scent of the heliotropes. I make a rapid mental note: cloying perfume, widow's purple, put in when describing summer evening. I catch us both up at every phrase, at every word, and I hasten to lock all these words and phrases away in my literary larder – you never know, they may come in handy! When I finish work I rush off to the theatre, or I go fishing; there at least I might relax and forget myself – but no, because inside my head a heavy iron ball is already beginning to shift – a new idea, and already I can feel the pull of my desk, and I have to rush off to write, write, write again. And that's how it always is, always and always, and I have no peace from myself, and I feel that I'm eating up my own life – that to make the honey I give to some remote reader I'm gathering the sweetness from my own best flowers – that I'm picking the flowers themselves and trampling their roots. I surely must be mad! My friends and relations surely can't be treating me like a sane man! 'What are you writing? What are you going to give us next?' Always the same thing, over and over again, and I get the feeling that this constant attention from my friends, this praise, this admiration, is all nothing but a trick, that I'm being lied to like an invalid, and sometimes I'm afraid they're just about to creep up on me from behind, that they're going to seize me like the wretched clerk in that story of Gogol's and cart me off to the madhouse. And in the years when I was a beginner still, the years when I was young, the best years, my trade was one long torment to me. The young writer – particularly when he's not successful – feels clumsy, inept, and useless; his nerves are on edge; he can't stop himself hanging round people connected with literature and art; an unacknowledged and unnoticed figure who's afraid to look people in the eye, like a compulsive gambler with no money. I couldn't see my reader, but in my imagination, for some reason, he was always someone unfriendly and mistrustful. I was afraid of the public, I found it terrifying, and whenever I had a new play produced I saw everyone with dark hair as antagonistic, and everyone with fair hair as coldly indifferent. It was terrible! It was a torment!

NINA. But surely inspiration, and the actual process of creation, give you moments of elevation, moments of happiness?

TRIGORIN. Yes, they do. When I'm writing it's rather agreeable. And reading the proofs – that's agreeable. But . . . scarcely has something come off the press than I can't bear it – I can see it's all wrong, it's a mistake, it should never have been written at all – and I feel disappointed, I feel deeply worthless . . . (*Laughs.*) But the public reads it and says: 'Yes, it's charming, it's clever . . . Charming, but nowhere near Tolstoy.' Or: 'It's a fine piece of writing, but Turgenev's *Fathers and Children* is better.' To my dying day it will go on being merely charming and clever, charming and clever, and nothing more, and when I'm dead my friends will say as they pass my grave: 'There lies Trigorin. He was a good writer, but he wasn't as good as Turgenev.'

NINA. Forgive me, but I refuse to understand what you're saying. You've simply been spoiled by success.

TRIGORIN. What success? I've never given any pleasure to myself. I don't like myself as a writer. The worst thing is that

I go round in some kind of daze, and often I don't understand what it is I'm writing . . . I love this water here, the trees, the sky; I have a feeling for nature – it arouses this passion I have, the irresistible desire to write. But then of course I'm not just a landscape-painter; I'm a citizen as well – I love my country, I love the common people. I feel that if I'm a writer then I have some obligation to deal with the people, with their sufferings and their future, to deal with science and the rights of man and so on and so forth; and deal with it all I do, in haste, urged on and snapped at on all sides. I rush back and forth like a fox bayed by hounds. I can see that life and science are getting further and further ahead of me all the time, while I fall further and further behind, like a peasant missing a train. And in the end I feel that all I can write is landscapes, and that in everything else I'm false – false to the marrow of my bones.

NINA. You've been overworking, and you haven't the time or the taste to become aware of your own importance. You may be dissatisfied with yourself, but in other people's eyes you're a great and wonderful man! If I were a writer like you I should sacrifice my whole life to the crowd – but I should know all the time that their happiness lay purely in reaching up to me, and they'd drag my chariot in triumph through the streets.

TRIGORIN. Dragging people in chariots, well . . . Agamemnon now, am I?

They both smile.

NINA. For the happiness of being a writer or an actress I'd put up with hunger and disappointment, and my family turning their backs on me. I'd live in a garret and eat black bread, I'd endure my dissatisfaction with myself and my consciousness of my own shortcomings; but then to make up for it I should demand glory . . . real resounding glory . . . (*Covers her face with her hands.*) My head's spinning . . . Oh . . . !

ARKADINA (*calls, off, from the house*). Boris! Boris?

TRIGORIN. I'm being summoned . . . Time to pack, I suppose. I don't feel like leaving, though. (*Looks around at the lake.*) Just look at the bounteousness of it . . . ! How fine!

NINA. You see the house and garden on the other side?

TRIGORIN. Yes.

NINA. My mother's dead now, but that was her estate. I was born there. I've spent my whole life around this lake – I know every little island in it.

TRIGORIN. A fine place you live in! (*Sees the seagull.*) What's that?

NINA. A seagull. Konstantin shot it.

TRIGORIN. Beautiful bird. I really don't feel like leaving. Why don't you try to persuade her to stay? (*Makes a note in his book.*)

NINA. What's that you're writing?

TRIGORIN. Nothing. Just jotting something down . . . An idea came into my head . . . (*Hides the book.*) An idea for a short story. A girl like you, living beside a lake since she was a child. She loves the lake the way a seagull might – she's as happy and free as a seagull. But one day by chance a man comes along and sees her. And quite idly he destroys her, like this seagull.

> *Pause.*
> ARKADINA *appears at the window.*

ARKADINA. Boris! Where are you?

TRIGORIN. Coming! (*Crosses to her, turning round to look at* NINA. *At the window, to* ARKADINA.) What is it?

ARKADINA. We're staying.

> *Exit* ARKADINA *into the house.*

NINA (*comes downstage and reflects for a moment*). A dream!

CURTAIN

Act Three

The dining-room in SORIN's *house. Doors left and right. Sideboard. Medicine cabinet. Dining-table in the middle of the room. Suitcase and cardboard boxes; signs of preparations for departure.* TRIGORIN *is eating lunch.* MASHA *is standing at the table.*

MASHA. I'm telling you all this because you're a writer. You can use it in something. Quite seriously, if he had wounded himself badly I couldn't have gone on living for another moment. I've got courage, though. I thought, 'Right!' – and I made up my mind to tear this love out of my heart, to tear it out by the roots.

TRIGORIN. How?

MASHA. I'm going to get married. To Medvedenko.

TRIGORIN. The schoolteacher?

MASHA. Yes.

TRIGORIN. I don't see the need for that.

MASHA. Loving without hope, waiting year after year for something to happen . . . I'm certainly not marrying for love, but I'll have new troubles to drown out the old. Be a change, anyway. Have another one, shall we?

TRIGORIN. Won't that be rather a lot?

MASHA. Oh, come on! (*Pours a glass each.*) There's no need to look at me like that. Women are more often drinkers than you realise. A few of them drink openly, like me, but most of them do it in secret. Oh yes. And always vodka or brandy. (*Clinks glasses.*) Here's to you! There's no nonsense about you – I'll be sorry to see you go.

They drink.

TRIGORIN. I don't much want to go myself.

MASHA. Ask her to stay, then.

TRIGORIN. No, she won't stay now. Her son's being extremely awkward. First he was trying to shoot himself; now, so I gather, he's going to challenge me to a duel. I don't know what for. He huffs and puffs, he preaches his 'new forms' . . . But there's room for all, surely, new and old alike – there's no need to elbow each other aside.

MASHA. How about jealousy? Not that it's any business of mine.

> *Pause.* YAKOV *crosses left to right with a suitcase.* NINA *enters and stops by the window.*

My schoolteacher isn't very clever, but he's a kind man, and he's poor, and he's very much in love with me. I feel sorry for him. I even feel sorry for his old mother. Anyway, let me wish you all the best. Remember me kindly. (*Shakes his hand warmly.*) I'm very grateful to you for taking an interest. Send me your books, though – and you must sign them! Don't put what you put for everybody else. Put 'To Masha, of dubious descent, and resident in this world for reasons unknown.' Goodbye!

> *Exit* MASHA.

NINA (*holding out a hand closed into a fist towards* TRIGORIN). Odds or evens?

TRIGORIN. Evens.

NINA (*sighs*). No. I've only got one bean in my hand. The question was, 'Should I become an actress or not?' If only someone could tell me!

TRIGORIN. It's not something that anyone *can* tell you.

NINA. We're saying goodbye to each other and . . . we may never see each other again. I should like to give you this little medallion to remember me by. I've had your initials engraved on it . . . and on this side the title of your book, *Days and Nights.*

TRIGORIN. What a very gracious gesture! (*Kisses the medallion.*)

It's a delightful present!

NINA. Remember me sometimes.

TRIGORIN. I shall remember you. I shall remember you as you were on that bright and sunny day – do you recall? – a week ago, when you were wearing a summer dress . . . and we had a talk . . . and there on the garden seat lay a white seagull.

NINA (*reflectively*). The seagull, yes . . . (*Pause.*) We can't say anything else – there are people coming . . . Give me two minutes before you leave, I beg of you.

> *She goes off left. As she does so* ARKADINA *enters right with* SORIN, *who is wearing a tailcoat with a decoration pinned to it, then* YAKOV, *who is preoccupied with collecting things up for the departure.*

ARKADINA. Now, why don't you stay at home, you poor old man? What do you want to go traipsing round calling on people for, with your rheumatism? (*To* TRIGORIN.) Who was that went out just now? Was that Nina?

TRIGORIN. Yes.

ARKADINA. *Pardon*, we're intruding . . . (*Sits.*) I think I've packed everything. What a torment it is.

TRIGORIN (*reads from the medallion*). *Days and Nights*, page 121, lines 11 and 12.

YAKOV (*clearing things from the table*). Am I to pack the fishing-rods, too?

TRIGORIN. Yes, I shall need them again. The books you can give away, though.

YAKOV. Sir.

TRIGORIN (*to himself*). Page 121, lines 11 and 12. What do they say? (*To* ARKADINA.) Have you got my books in the house?

ARKADINA. My brother's study – the corner cupboard.

TRIGORIN. Page 121 . . .

> *Exit* TRIGORIN.

ARKADINA. Really, Petrusha, I should stay at home if I

were you . . . .

SORIN. You're leaving. I shall get depressed sitting at home without you.

ARKADINA. What's happening in town, then?

SORIN. Nothing much, but all the same. (*Laughs.*) They're laying the foundation-stone for the new government building, etcetera, etcetera . . . I'd like to get out and about for an hour or two, anyway – I've been lying here like an old boot, stuck here like a gudgeon in the mud. I've ordered the horses for one o'clock, we can go together.

ARKADINA (*after a pause*). Well, you go on living here, then – don't get too bored, don't catch any colds. Keep an eye on my son. Look after him. Admonish him. (*Pause.*) I'm leaving, so I'll never know why Konstantin tried to shoot himself. The main reason, I think, was jealousy, and the sooner I take Trigorin away from here the better.

SORIN. I don't know quite how to put this, but there were other reasons, too. There he is, no question about it – young man, intelligent, he lives in the country, miles from anywhere, and he's no money, no position, no future. Nothing to do. He's ashamed of his idleness – he's frightened of it. I'm devoted to him and he's quite attached to me, but when all's said and done he feels there's no place for him in the house – he feels like a poor relation here, a parasite. Pride, no question about it . . .

ARKADINA. Oh, he's a trial to me! (*Lost in thought.*) Maybe he should get a job . . .

SORIN (*whistles for a moment, then, irresolutely*). I wonder if the best thing wouldn't be for you to . . . give him a little money. The first thing he needs to do is to dress like a normal human being, it's as simple as that. Look, he's been wearing that one same jacket for the past three years. He hasn't got an overcoat to his back . . . . (*Laughs.*) Then again it wouldn't hurt the boy to see a bit of the world . . . Go abroad, perhaps . . . It really wouldn't cost all that much.

ARKADINA. All the same . . . I suppose I might arrange a little
    more for clothes, but as for going abroad . . . No, at the
    moment I can't even manage the clothes. (*Decisively.*) I've no
    money!

SORIN *laughs.*

I haven't!

SORIN (*whistles for a moment*). Well, there we are. Forgive me.
    Don't be angry, my dear. I believe you . . . You're a good and
    generous woman.

ARKADINA (*on the verge of tears*). I've no money!

SORIN. If I had any money, no question, I'd give him some
    myself, but I've nothing, not a kopeck. (*Laughs.*) My entire
    pension is taken by that steward of mine to spend on planting
    crops and raising cattle and keeping bees, and I might as well
    pour it straight down the drain. The bees drop dead, the cows
    drop dead, and they never let me have any horses . . .

ARKADINA. All right, I have money, but I happen to be in the
    theatrical profession – my outfits alone have nearly ruined
    me.

SORIN. You're a dear kind girl . . . I respect your feelings . . .
    Yes . . . But I think I'm having another of my . . . you know
    . . . (*Staggers.*) Head's going round. (*Holds on to the table.*)
    Not feeling too good, simple as that.

ARKADINA (*frightened*). Petrusha! (*Trying to support him.*)
    Petrusha, my dear . . . (*Calls.*) Help me! Help . . . !

    Enter KONSTANTIN, *his head bandaged, and*
    MEDVEDENKO.

ARKADINA. He's ill!

SORIN. I'm all right, I'm all right . . . (*Smiles and drinks some
    water.*) It's passed off . . . simple as that . . .

KONSTANTIN (*to his mother*). There's no need to be frightened,
    Mama, it's not dangerous. Uncle often has these turns now.
    Uncle, you must have a lie-down.

SORIN. For a moment, yes . . . I'm still going into town. I'll
have a little lie-down, then I'll go . . . no question about
it . . .

He begins to go off, leaning on his stick.

MEDVEDENKO (*taking his arm*). There's a riddle: in the
morning on four, at midday on two, in the evening on
three . . .

SORIN (*laughs*). Quite. And at night on your back. Thank you
– I can manage on my own . . .

MEDVEDENKO. Well, there's politeness . . .

Exeunt MEDVEDENKO *and* SORIN.

ARKADINA. He gave me such a fright!

KONSTANTIN. It's bad for his health, living in the country.
He's pining away. Now, Mama, if you had a sudden attack
of generosity and lent him a couple of thousand rubles he
could live in town all year.

ARKADINA. I haven't any money. I'm an actress, not a bank-
manager.

Pause.

KONSTANTIN. Will you change my dressing, Mama. You do
it so nicely.

ARKADINA (*gets iodoform and dressings out of the medicine
cabinet*). The doctor's late, though.

KONSTANTIN. He promised to be here at ten, and it's twelve
already.

ARKADINA. Sit down. (*Takes the bandage off his head.*) You
look as if you're wearing a turban. Someone who came to the
kitchen door yesterday was asking what nationality you were.
It's nearly healed, though. Only the merest trifle left to go.
(*Kisses him on the head.*) You're not going to start playing with
guns again while I'm away, are you.

KONSTANTIN. No, Mama. That was just a moment of crazy

despair when I lost control of myself. It won't happen again. (*Kisses her hand.*) You have magic in your hands. I remember a long time ago, when you were still working in the State theatre – when I was little – there was a fight in the courtyard of our block, and a washerwoman living in one of the apartments got badly knocked about. Do you remember? When they picked her up she was unconscious . . . You kept going to see her, you took her medicine, you bathed the children in her washtub. Surely you remember?

ARKADINA. No. (*Puts a new bandage on.*)

KONSTANTIN. There were two ballet-dancers living in the same block . . . They used to come and have coffee with you . . .

ARKADINA. I remember that.

KONSTANTIN. They were terribly religious. (*Pause.*) These last few days I've loved you as tenderly and whole-heartedly as I did when I was a child. I've no one left apart from you. But why, why has that man come between us?

ARKADINA. Konstantin, you don't understand him. He's someone of the highest integrity . . .

KONSTANTIN. However, when they told him I was going to challenge him to a duel his integrity didn't hinder his cowardice. He's leaving. Ignominiously fleeing!

ARKADINA. Oh, nonsense! I'm taking him away. You can't be pleased by our relationship, of course, but you're perfectly intelligent, and I must insist that you respect my freedom.

KONSTANTIN. I do respect your freedom, but you must allow me to be free, too, you must let me have my own opinion of that man. Someone of the highest integrity! Here we are on the point of quarrelling over him while he sits in the drawing-room or the garden somewhere laughing at us . . . Educating Nina, trying to convince her once and for all that he's a genius.

ARKADINA. You take pleasure in being disagreeable to me. That man is someone I have great respect for, and I must ask you not to speak ill of him in my presence.

KONSTANTIN. I don't have great respect for him, however. You want me to think he's a genius as well, but I'm sorry, I can't tell a lie – his work nauseates me.

ARKADINA. That's jealousy. People with no talent themselves, only pretensions, are always reduced to running down people who do have real talent. It must be a great comfort!

KONSTANTIN (*ironically*). Real talent! (*Furiously.*) I've more talent than the lot of you, if it comes to that! (*Tears the bandage off his head.*) You and your dull, plodding friends have got a stranglehold on art, and the only things you consider legitimate and real are the ones you do yourselves – everything else you crush and smother! I don't acknowledge any of you! I don't acknowledge you, I don't acknowledge him!

ARKADINA. And what are you? A Decadent!

KONSTANTIN. Go off to your nice little theatre and act in your miserable mediocre plays!

ARKADINA. I've never acted in plays like that in my life! Leave me alone! You couldn't write so much as a miserable farce! You shopkeeper! Yes – Kiev shopkeeper! Parasite!

KONSTANTIN. Miser!

ARKADINA. Ragbag!

KONSTANTIN *sits down and weeps quietly.*

Nonentity! (*Passing to agitation.*) Don't cry. There's no need to cry . . . (*Weeps.*) You mustn't cry . . . (*Kisses him on his brow, his cheeks, his head.*) My own dear child, forgive me . . . Forgive your wicked mother. Forgive your unhappy mother.

KONSTANTIN (*embraces her*). If only you knew! I've lost everything. She doesn't love me, I can't write any more . . . All my hopes have foundered . . .

ARKADINA. Don't despair . . . Everything will be all right. I'm taking him away now – she'll go back to loving you. (*Wipes his tears.*) Enough, enough. We're friends again.

KONSTANTIN (*kisses her hands*). Yes, Mama.

ARKADINA (*gently*). Be friends with him, too. No duels . . . You won't, will you?

KONSTANTIN. Very well . . . But please, Mama, I don't want to meet him. It's hard for me . . . more than I can bear . . .

   Enter TRIGORIN.

So . . . I'm going . . . (*Quickly puts the medical supplies back in the cabinet.*) The doctor can do the dressing later . . .

TRIGORIN (*searches in a book*). Page 121 . . . Lines 11 and 12 . . . Here we are . . . (*Reads.*) 'If ever you have need of my life, then come and take it.'

   KONSTANTIN *picks up the bandage from the floor and goes out.*

ARKADINA (*glancing at the clock*). They'll be bringing the horses very shortly.

TRIGORIN (*to himself*). If ever you have need of my life, then come and take it.

ARKADINA. You're packed, I hope?

TRIGORIN (*impatiently*). Yes, yes . . . (*Lost in thought.*) Why do I hear a note of sadness in that cry from a pure heart, and why has my own heart so painfully contracted . . . ? If ever you have need of my life, then come and take it. (*To* ARKADINA.) Let's stop another day!

   ARKADINA *shakes her head.*

Just one more day!

ARKADINA. My dear, I know what keeps you here. But do take a hold of yourself. You're a little intoxicated – you must be sober again.

TRIGORIN. You must be sober, too – be understanding and sensible, I implore you – see all this like the true friend you are . . . (*Presses her hand.*) You're capable of sacrifice . . . Be my friend – let me go . . .

ARKADINA (*in great agitation*). You're as captivated as that?

TRIGORIN. I feel as if a voice were calling me to her! Perhaps this is the very thing I need.

ARKADINA. Some provincial girl's love? How little you understand yourself!

TRIGORIN. Sometimes people fall asleep on their feet – and that's how I am now, talking to you but feeling all the time as if I were asleep and dreaming of her . . . Sweet and marvellous dreams have taken hold of me . . . Let me go . . .

ARKADINA (*trembling*). No, no . . . I'm a woman like any other – you can't speak to me so . . . Don't torment me, Boris . . . It frightens me . . .

TRIGORIN. If you choose you can be a woman unlike any other. A young love – a love full of charm and poetry – bearing me off into the land of dreams . . . in all this wide world no one but her can give me happiness! The sort of love I've never known yet . . . I'd no time for it when I was young, when I was beating on editors' doors, when I was struggling with poverty . . . Now here it is, that love I never knew – it's come, it's calling to me . . . What sense in running away from it?

ARKADINA (*with fury*). You've gone mad!

TRIGORIN. Release me, then.

ARKADINA. You've all conspired to torment me today! (*Weeps.*)

TRIGORIN (*clutches his head*). She doesn't understand! She won't understand!

ARKADINA. Am I really so old and ugly that you can talk to me about other women without so much as batting an eyelid? (*Embraces and kisses him.*) Oh, you're out of your senses! My wonderful man, my marvellous man . . . The last page of my life! (*Kneels.*) My joy, my pride, my delight . . . (*Embraces his knees.*) Leave me for a single hour and I'll never survive it, I'll go mad, my amazing man, my magnificent man, my sovereign lord . . .

TRIGORIN. Someone may come in. (*Helps her to her feet.*)

ARKADINA. Let them – I'm not ashamed of my love for you. (*Kisses his hands.*) My treasure, my wild and desperate man, you want to behave like a lunatic, but I don't want you to, I won't let you . . . (*Laughs.*) You're mine . . . you're mine . . . This brow of yours is mine, these eyes are mine, this lovely silken hair is mine . . . You're all mine. You're such a talented man, such an intelligent man, you're the finest writer alive today, you're the sole hope of Russia . . . You have so much sincerity, so much simplicity and freshness and wholesome humour . . . With one stroke you're able to convey the essence of a person or a landscape, your characters live and breathe. Impossible to read you without delight! You think this is mere incense at your altar? That I'm flattering you? Look into my eyes . . . look into them . . . Do I look like a liar? See for yourself – I'm the only one who can appreciate you, the only one who tells you the truth, my sweet, my marvel . . . You'll come away? Yes? You won't abandon me . . . ?

TRIGORIN. I've no will of my own . . . I've never had a will of my own . . . Flabby, crumbling, endlessly submissive – is that really what pleases a woman? Pick me up, carry me off – just don't let me out of your sight for an instant.

ARKADINA (*to herself*). Now he's mine. (*Easily, as if nothing had happened*). Anyway, you can stay if you like. I'll go, and you can come on later, in a week's time. There's really no reason for you to hurry, is there?

TRIGORIN. No, no, we'll go together.

ARKADINA. Whichever you like. Together – all right, together . . .

Pause. TRIGORIN *notes something down in his book.*

What's that?

TRIGORIN. I heard a rather nice turn of phrase this morning – 'Virgins' forest . . .' Might come in handy. (*Stretches.*) So, we're going to be travelling? Stations and carriages again, station restaurants and station cutlets, conversations on trains . . .

Enter SHAMRAYEV.

SHAMRAYEV. I have to inform you, with the utmost regret, that the horses are ready. It's time, dear lady, to go to the station; the train arrives at five minutes after two. Now you won't forget, if you will be so kind, to inquire into the whereabouts of that actor, Suzdaltzev? Is he alive and well? We used to go drinking together once upon a time . . . His performance in *The Great Mail Robbery* was beyond compare . . . At that time, as I recall, he was working with the tragedian Izmailov – another remarkable character . . . Don't hurry yourself, dear lady, another five minutes yet. Once, in some melodrama, they were playing conspirators, and when they were suddenly discovered he was supposed to say: 'Caught, like rats in a trap!' Izmailov – 'Caught, like trats in a rap!' (*Laughs.*) Trats in a rap!

While he has been speaking, YAKOV *has been busy with the suitcases, the* MAID *has been bringing* ARKADINA *her hat, coat, umbrella, and gloves, and everyone has been helping her to put her things on. The* MAN COOK *has looked in from the lefthand door, and then a few moments later come uncertainly all the way in. Enter* POLINA, *followed later by* SORIN *and* MEDVEDENKO.

POLINA (*offering a punnet*). Some plums for the journey . . . They're very sweet. You might feel like something nice . . .

ARKADINA. That's very kind of you.

POLINA. Goodbye, my dear. If anything was not as it should have been then please forgive me. (*Weeps.*)

ARKADINA (*embraces her*). Everything was fine, everything was fine. Only you mustn't start crying.

POLINA. Our lives are running out!

ARKADINA. But what can we do?

> SORIN, *wearing hat and Inverness, and carrying a stick, comes out of the lefthand door and crosses the room.*

SORIN. Time to go. You don't want to be late, when all's said and done. I'm going to get in.

> *Exit* SORIN.

MEDVEDENKO. Yes, and I'm going to walk to the station . . . See you off. I'll have to look sharp . . .

> *Exit* MEDVEDENKO.

ARKADINA. Goodbye, then, my dears . . . We'll see each other again next summer, if we're spared . . .

> *The* MAID, YAKOV, *and the* COOK *kiss her hand.*

Don't forget me.

> *Gives the* COOK *a ruble.*

Here, a ruble. That's for all three of you.

COOK. Thank you kindly, ma'am. Have a good journey, now! Very grateful to you!

YAKOV. God send you good fortune!

SHAMRAYEV. Give us the pleasure of hearing from you! (*To* TRIGORIN.) Goodbye, then.

ARKADINA. Where's Konstantin? Will you tell him I'm going? I must say goodbye to him. Well, then, remember me kindly. (*To* YAKOV.) I gave cook a ruble. That's for all three of you.

> *They all go off right. The stage is empty. Noises off, of the sort that occur when people are being said goodbye to. The* MAID *comes back and takes the basket of plums off the table, then goes out again.* TRIGORIN *comes back in.*

TRIGORIN. I've forgotten my stick. I think it's out on the verandah.

Crosses towards the lefthand door and meets NINA *as she enters.*

There you are. We're leaving.

NINA. I had a feeling we'd see each other again. (*Excitedly.*) I've made up my mind, once and for all – I'm going on the stage. By tomorrow I shan't be here – I'm getting away from my father, I'm abandoning everything, I'm starting a new life . . . I'm leaving, just like you . . . for Moscow. We shall see each other there.

TRIGORIN (*looking round*). Stay at the Slavyansky Bazar . . . Let me know as soon as you arrive . . . Grokholsky's house, on Molchanovka . . . I must hurry . . .

Pause

NINA. Another minute . . .

TRIGORIN (*keeping his voice down*). You're so lovely . . . Oh, what joy it is to think we shall be seeing each other again before long!

She lays her head against his chest.

I shall see those marvellous eyes again, this inexpressibly lovely, tender smile . . . these gentle features, this look of angelic innocence . . . My dear . . .

A prolonged kiss.

CURTAIN

Handwritten annotations in margins:
- windy sounds
- trees brushing
- key rattle
- watchman's
- shuttle slamming
- into
- switch turns

Act Four

Two years have elapsed.

One of the reception-rooms in SORIN's *house which* KONSTANTIN *has turned into a working study. Doors left and right leading to inner rooms. A glass door, centre, opening on to the verandah. Apart from the usual living-room furniture there is a writing table in the righthand corner, a Turkish divan beside the lefthand door, a cupboard full of books, and more books on the window-ledges and chairs. – Evening. A single shaded lamp is alight. Twilight. The sighing of the trees can be heard, and the howling of the wind in the chimneys. The sound of the watchman's rattle as he passes. Enter* MEDVEDENKO *and* MASHA.

MASHA (*calls*). Hello? Are you there? (*Looks round.*) No one. The old man keeps asking every minute, 'Where's Kostya? Where's Konstantin?' He can't live without him . . .

MEDVEDENKO. He's frightened of being alone. (*Listens.*) What terrible weather! All yesterday, too, all last night.

MASHA (*turns up the lamp*). There are waves on the lake. Huge waves.

MEDVEDENKO. The garden's quite dark. They should tell someone to knock down that theatre. It's as hideous as bare bones, and the curtain slaps in the wind. When I was going past yesterday evening I could have sworn there was someone crying in there.

MASHA. Well, then . . .

Pause.

MEDVEDENKO. Let's go home, Masha!

MASHA (*shakes her head*). I'm staying the night.

MEDVEDENKO (*pleading*). Masha, let's go! The baby could be

hungry, who knows?

MASHA. Oh, fiddle. Matryona will feed him.

Pause.

MEDVEDENKO. It's a shame, though. This will be his third night without his mother.

MASHA. What a bore you've become. At least it was philosophical vapourings before – now it's the baby and let's go home all the time, the baby and let's go home – I never hear anything else out of you.

MEDVEDENKO. Let's go, Masha!

MASHA. You go.

MEDVEDENKO. Your father won't give me any horses.

MASHA. Yes, he will. Just ask him – he'll give you some.

MEDVEDENKO. Well, perhaps I'll ask him. So you'll be coming tomorrow?

MASHA (*takes a pinch of snuff*). Yes, yes, tomorrow. You keep badgering away . . .

Enter KONSTANTIN *and* POLINA. KONSTANTIN *has brought pillows and a blanket, and* POLINA *bed-linen. They put all this on the Turkish divan, then* KONSTANTIN *crosses to his desk and sits down.*

What's that for, Mama?

POLINA. He's asked to have a bed made up for him in here with Konstantin.

MASHA. I'll do it . . . (*She makes up the bed.*)

POLINA (*sighs*). Second childhood . . . (*Crosses to the writing table, rests her elbows on it, and looks at a manuscript. Pause.*)

MEDVEDENKO. I'll be off, then. Goodbye, Masha. (*Kisses his wife's hand.*) Goodbye, Mother. (*Tries to kiss his mother-in-law's hand.*)

POLINA (*with annoyance*). Oh, come on, now! Off you go.

MEDVEDENKO (*to* KONSTANTIN). Goodbye, then.

KONSTANTIN *proffers his hand in silence. Exit* MEDVEDENKO.

POLINA (*looking at the manuscript*). No one ever dreamed you'd turn out to be a real writer, Kostya. But now, thanks be to God, you've even started to get money from those literary magazines. (*Runs her hand through his hair.*) You've turned into a handsome man, too . . . Dear Kostya, be a good boy, now, and be a bit kinder to my poor Masha . . . !

MASHA (*making the bed*). Leave him, Mama.

POLINA (*to* KONSTANTIN). She's a sweet, good girl. (*Pause.*) All a woman needs, Kostya, is the odd kind glance. I know from my own experience.

KONSTANTIN *gets up from his desk and silently leaves the room.*

MASHA. Now you've put his back up. What did you have to go badgering him for?

POLINA. I feel sorry for you, Masha.

MASHA. A lot of help that is.

POLINA. My heart aches for you. Do you think I can't see what's happening? Do you think I don't understand?

MASHA. It's all nonsense. Love without hope – that's just in novels. Fiddle! You mustn't lose your grip on yourself, that's all, you mustn't keep waiting for something to happen, like a sailor waiting for the weather . . . Once love has dug itself into your heart you have to get it out again. They've promised to transfer my husband to another district. As soon as we've got there I shall forget it all . . . I shall tear it out of my heart by the roots.

A melancholy waltz can be heard from the next room but one.

POLINA. That's Kostya playing. He's down in the dumps, then.

MASHA (*noiselessly performs one or two turns of the waltz*). The main thing, Mama, is not to have him in front of my eyes all the time. Just let them give Semyon his transfer and, believe me, in a month I shall have forgotten him. So fiddle-de-dee.

> *The lefthand door opens.* SORIN, *in his wheelchair, is pushed in by* DORN *and* MEDVEDENKO.

MEDVEDENKO. I've got six of us at home now. With flour at two kopecks a pound.

DORN. You'll just have to manage.

MEDVEDENKO. Yes, you can laugh. You've got plenty of money.

DORN. Money? In thirty years of practice, my friend, thirty years of unrelenting practice, when night and day I couldn't call my soul my own, I managed to save a miserable two thousand rubles – and even that I went through while I was abroad just now. I've nothing.

MASHA (*to her husband*). Haven't you gone?

MEDVEDENKO (*guiltily*). How can I? When they won't give me any horses!

MASHA (*with bitter irritation, lowering her voice*). I just want you out of my sight!

> *The wheelchair comes to a halt in the lefthand half of the room.* POLINA, MASHA, *and* DORN *sit down beside it.* MEDVEDENKO *moves sadly aside.*

DORN. So many changes here, though! You've turned this drawing-room into a study.

MASHA. It's more convenient for Konstantin, working in here. He can go out into the garden to think whenever he feels like it.

> *The watchman's rattle, off.*

SORIN. Where's my sister?

DORN. Gone to the station to meet Trigorin. Back in a moment.

SORIN. If you thought it necessary to get my sister here then

I must be dangerously ill. (*Falls silent for a moment.*) A fine business, I must say – here I am, dangerously ill, and they won't give me any medicine.

DORN. What would you like, then? Valerian drops? Bicarbonate of soda? Quinine?

SORIN. Yes, and now we get the moralising. Oh, what a penance it is! (*Nodding at the divan.*) Is that made up for me?

POLINA. For you, yes.

SORIN. Thank you.

    DORN *hums to himself.*

Now, I should like to give Kostya an idea for a story. It would be entitled: *The Man who wanted to.* Once, when I was young, I wanted to become a man of letters – and I never became one. I wanted to speak well – and I've always spoken appallingly. (*Mimics himself.*) 'Simple as that, etcetera etcetera . . . I mean . . . you know . . .' – I used to drag out a summing-up to such lengths I'd break into a sweat. I wanted to get married – and I never got married. I wanted always to live in town – and here I am ending my days in the country, simple as that.

DORN. You wanted to get to the fourth grade of the civil service – and you did.

SORIN (*laughs*). I wasn't trying for that. That came of its own accord.

DORN. Come now, giving vent to your dissatisfaction with life at the age of sixty-two is not very handsome.

SORIN. It's like talking to the gatepost. Can't you get it into your head that I want to live?

DORN. That's fatuous. According to the laws of nature every life must have an end.

SORIN. You speak as someone who's eaten his fill. You've had your fill so you're indifferent to life – it's all one to you. But even you will dread to die.

DORN. The dread of death is an animal dread . . . It has to be suppressed. The only people who can rationally fear death are the ones who believe in eternal life, and who dread for their sins. But firstly, you're an unbeliever, and secondly – what are your sins? You served twenty-five years in the Department of Justice, that's all!

SORIN (*laughs*). Twenty-eight . . .

Enter KONSTANTIN. *He sits down on a stool at* SORIN's *feet.* MASHA *does not take her eyes off him all the time he is there.*

DORN. We're stopping Konstantin from working.

KONSTANTIN. No, it's all right.

Pause.

MEDVEDENKO. May I ask you, Doctor, which foreign city you liked best?

DORN. Genoa.

KONSTANTIN. Why Genoa?

DORN. There's a splendid street life there. When you come out of your hotel in the evening the whole street is jammed with people. You wander aimlessly about in the crowd, hither and thither, this way that way, and you share its life, you spiritually merge with it. You begin to believe that it would in fact be possible to have a single world soul of the sort that your friend Nina once acted in your play. Where is she now, by the way? Where is she and how is she?

KONSTANTIN. She's well, as far as I know.

DORN. I heard she was leading some strange sort of life. What's it all about?

KONSTANTIN. It's a long story, Doctor.

DORN. In a nutshell.

Pause.

KONSTANTIN. She ran away from home and took up with Trigorin. You know that much?

DORN. I know that much.

KONSTANTIN. She had a child. The child died. Trigorin decided he was no longer in love with her and reverted to his former attachment, as was only to be expected. Not that he'd ever given it up. Being the spineless creature that he is he'd somehow contrived to keep a foothold in both camps. So far as I can make out, Nina's private life has not been a total success.

DORN. How about the stage?

KONSTANTIN. Even worse, I think. She made her debut at a summer theatre somewhere outside Moscow, and then went to the provinces. I wasn't letting her out of my sight at that point, and for some time wherever she went I went, too. She kept taking on big parts, but she played them crudely and vulgarly, with a lot of howling and sawing of the air. There were moments when she showed some talent in shouting, or dying, but they were only moments.

DORN. So there is talent there, at any rate?

KONSTANTIN. It was difficult to tell. There probably is. I could see her, but she wouldn't see me, and her maid would never let me into her room. I undertood her feelings, and I didn't insist. (*Pause.*) What else can I tell you? When I was home again I started getting letters from her. Intelligent, warm, interesting letters. She never complained, but I could sense that she was deeply unhappy, that there was a sick nervous strain in every line. Even her imagination was a little distraught. She'd sign herself 'The Seagull'. It was like that play of Pushkin's where the old miller goes mad with grief and says he's a raven. She kept saying in the letters that she was a seagull. Now she's here.

DORN. How do you mean, here?

KONSTANTIN. In town, at the inn. She's been living in a room there for the best part of a week. I'd have gone to call on her – in fact Masha here did go – but she won't see anyone. Semyon says he saw her yesterday evening, in the fields a mile or so from here.

MEDVEDENKO. Yes, I did. She was going away from here, towards town. I said hello to her and asked why she didn't come to see us. She said she would.

KONSTANTIN. She won't, though. (*Pause.*) Her father and stepmother have disowned her. They've put watchmen everywhere to stop her even getting near the estate.

Crosses to his writing-table with the doctor.

How easy it is, Doctor, to be a philosopher on paper, and how difficult to be one in real life!

SORIN. She was a delightful girl.

DORN. I beg your pardon?

SORIN. I said she was a delightful girl. One former civil servant of the fourth grade was even in love with her for a while.

DORN. You old rake.

SHAMRAYEV laughs, off.

POLINA. It sounds as if they've arrived from the station.

KONSTANTIN. Yes, I can hear Mama.

Enter ARKADINA and TRIGORIN, followed by SHAMRAYEV.

SHAMRAYEV (*as he enters*). We're all getting older, we're all getting a little weather-beaten – but you, dear lady, go on being young . . . Dressed in light colours, full of life and grace . . .

ARKADINA. You're tempting fortune again, you tiresome man!

TRIGORIN (*to SORIN*). Hello! Still not better, then? We can't have that! (*Joyfully, at the sight of MASHA.*) And you're here!

MASHA. You recognised me, then? (*Shakes hands.*)

TRIGORIN. Married?

MASHA. Long since.

TRIGORIN. Happy?

He exchanges bows with DORN and MEDVEDENKO, then goes uncertainly up to KONSTANTIN.

I'm told you're ready to let bygones be bygones.

KONSTANTIN *holds out his hand.*

ARKADINA (*to her son*). He's brought the magazine with your new story.

KONSTANTIN (*to* TRIGORIN, *taking the volume*). Thank you. Most kind.

They sit.

TRIGORIN. I bring greetings from all your admirers. You're the talk of Petersburg and Moscow alike, and people keep asking me about you. They want to know what sort of person you are – how old – are you fair or are you dark? They all think you're middle-aged, I don't know why. And no one knows your real name, since you always publish under a pen-name. You're as mysterious as the Man in the Iron Mask.

KONSTANTIN. Are you here for long?

TRIGORIN. No, I'm leaving for Moscow tomorrow. I have to. I'm rushing to finish a story, and then I've promised something for a collection. Life as ever, in a word.

While they are talking, ARKADINA *and* POLINA *are setting up a card-table in the middle of the room and putting a cloth on it.* SHAMRAYEV *is lighting the candles and setting chairs. They get a lotto set out of the cupboard.*

Not a very warm welcome from the weather. A cruel wind. In the morning, if it drops, I'm going down to the lake for some fishing. I must take a look at the garden as I go, and the spot where your play was performed – do you remember? I've been developing an idea for a story. I just need to refresh my memory of the setting.

MASHA (*to her father*). Let my husband take a horse! He's got to get home.

SHAMRAYEV (*mimics her*). Horse . . . home . . . (*Sternly.*) You know as well as I do – they've just been out to the station.

They can't go running all over the countryside again.

MASHA. There *are* other horses . . . (*Sees that her father is not responding and flaps her hand.*) Oh, what's the use . . . ?

MEDVEDENKO. Masha, I'll walk. Really . . .

POLINA (*sighs*). Walk, in weather like this . . . (*Sits down at the card-table.*) Come on, then, everyone.

MEDVEDENKO. I mean, it's only three miles or so . . . Goodbye . . . (*Kisses his wife's hand.*) Goodbye, Mother. (*His mother-in-law reluctantly gives him her hand to be kissed.*) I wouldn't disturb anyone, only it's the baby . . . (*Bows to everyone.*) Goodbye . . .

Exit MEDVEDENKO, *with apologetic gait.*

SHAMRAYEV. I dare say he'll manage it. He's not a general.

POLINA (*raps on the table*). Come on, then. Let's not waste time – they'll be calling us for supper in a minute.

SHAMRAYEV, MASHA, *and* DORN *sit down at the table.*

ARKADINA (*to* TRIGORIN). When the long autumn evenings come they play lotto here. Look – an antique set that we used when our poor mother played with us as children. Won't you try a round with us before supper?

Sits down with TRIGORIN *at the table.*

It's a boring game, but it's all right when you get used to it.

She gives everyone three cards each.

KONSTANTIN (*leafing through the magazine*). He's read his own story, and he hasn't even cut the pages of mine.

He puts the magazine down on his writing-table, then goes to the lefthand door. As he passes his mother he kisses her head.

ARKADINA. How about you, Kostya?

KONSTANTIN. Will you excuse me? I don't really feel like it . . . I'm going to walk up and down for a bit.

Exit KONSTANTIN.

ARKADINA. The stake is ten kopecks. Put in for me, will you, Doctor.

DORN. Ma'am.

MASHA. Has everyone put in? I'm starting . . . Twenty-two!

ARKADINA. Yes.

MASHA. Three!

DORN. Right.

MASHA. Have you put it on? Eighty-one! Ten!

SHAMRAYEV. Not so fast.

ARKADINA. Oh, but my dears, the reception I got in Kharkov! My head is still spinning!

MASHA. Thirty-four!

A melancholy waltz is played, off.

ARKADINA. The students gave me an ovation . . . Three baskets of flowers, two garlands, and this . . . (*Takes a brooch off her breast and throws it on to the table.*)

SHAMRAYEV. Oh, yes! Yes, indeed!

MASHA. Fifty . . . !

DORN. Fifty-what? Just fifty?

ARKADINA. I was wearing an amazing outfit . . . Whatever else, I do know how to dress.

POLINA. That's Kostya playing. The poor boy's pining.

SHAMRAYEV. They're being very rude about him in the papers.

MASHA. Seventy-seven!

ARKADINA. Why does he pay any attention?

TRIGORIN. He's not having much success. He still just can't find his own voice. There's something odd and formless about his work – something verging at times on the nightmarish. Never a single living character.

MASHA. Eleven!

ARKADINA (*glances at* SORIN). Petrusha, is this boring for you?

(*Pause.*) He's asleep.

DORN. One former civil servant of the fourth grade is fast asleep.

MASHA. Seven! Ninety!

TRIGORIN. If I'd lived on an estate like this, beside a lake, do you think I should ever have taken up writing? I should have wrestled the passion down, and done nothing but fish.

MASHA. Twenty-eight!

TRIGORIN. To catch a ruff or a perch – that is perfect happiness!

DORN. I believe in the boy, though. There's something there! There's something there! He thinks in images, his stories are bright and colourful, and they speak to me strongly. The only sad thing is that he doesn't have any clear aims. He produces an impression but nothing more, and you can't get all that far on impressions alone. (*To* ARKADINA.) Are you pleased to have a son who's a writer?

ARKADINA. Can you imagine, I still haven't read anything by him. I never have time.

MASHA. Twenty-six!

KONSTANTIN *comes quietly in and goes to his desk.*

SHAMRAYEV (*to* TRIGORIN). And we still have one of your things here.

TRIGORIN. What's that?

SHAMRAYEV. Konstantin somehow managed to shoot a seagull, and you told me to have it stuffed.

TRIGORIN. I don't remember that. (*Reflecting.*) No recollection!

MASHA. Sixty-six! One!

KONSTANTIN (*flings open the window and listens*). Pitch dark. I can't think why I feel so uneasy.

ARKADINA. Kostya, shut the window, there's a draft.

KONSTANTIN *shuts the window.*

MASHA. Eighty-eight!

TRIGORIN. Ladies and gentlemen, I have a full house.

ARKADINA (*merrily*). Bravo! Bravo!

SHAMRAYEV. Bravo!

ARKADINA. Always, wherever he goes, that man has all the luck. (*Gets up.*) Now let's go and have something to eat, though. Our visiting celebrity hasn't had a proper meal today. We'll go on again after supper. (*To her son.*) Kostya, leave your writing – let's go and eat.

KONSTANTIN. I won't, Mama. I'm not hungry.

ARKADINA. As you wish.

Wakes SORIN.

Petrusha – supper!

Takes SHAMRAYEV'*s arm.*

I'll tell you all about the reception I got in Kharkov . . .

POLINA *extinguishes the candles on the table, then she and* DORN *push the wheelchair. They all go out through the lefthand door.* KONSTANTIN *remains alone on stage at his writing table.*

KONSTANTIN (*about to write, runs through what he has written already*). I've talked so much about new forms, and now I feel I'm gradually slipping into the same old pattern myself. (*Reads*) 'The poster on the fence was announcing to the world . . . Her pale face, framed by her dark hair . . .' 'Announcing to the world . . .' 'framed . . .' It's undistinguished. (*Deletes.*) I'll start with the man being woken by the sound of the rain, and all the rest can go. The description of the moonlit night – that's long and laboured. Trigorin has developed his special little tricks – it's easy for him . . . He has the neck of a broken bottle glittering on the bank of the millpool and the shadow of the water-wheel black beside it – and there's his moonlit night set up; while I have the shimmering light, plus the silent twinkling of the stars, plus the distant sound of a piano fading in the silent scented air . . . It's excruciating. (*Pause.*) Yes, I'm coming more and more to the conclusion that it's not a question of forms, old or new, but of writing without thought to any forms at all − writing because it flows freely out of your heart.

Someone taps on the window nearest to the desk.

What was that? (*Looks out of the window.*) I can't see anything . . . (*Opens the glass door and looks into the garden.*) Someone running down the steps. (*Calls*) Who's there?

He goes out. He can be heard walking rapidly across the verandah. A moment later he comes back in with NINA.

Nina! Nina!

NINA *lays her head on his chest and sobs, trying to control herself.*

(*Moved*). Nina! Nina! It's you . . . it's you . . . I had a kind of premonition − my mind's been in a torment all day. (*Takes her hat and shawl.*) Oh, my dear girl, my love − she's come! We mustn't cry, we mustn't.

NINA. There's someone here.

KONSTANTIN. There's no one.

NINA. Lock the doors − someone may come in.

KONSTANTIN. No one's going to come in.

NINA. Your mother's here, I know. Lock the doors . . .

KONSTANTIN (*locks the righthand door with its key, then crosses to the lefthand door*). There's no lock on this one. I'll barricade it with the chair. (*Puts an armchair against the door.*) Don't worry, no one's going to come in now.

NINA (*gazes intently into his face*). Let me look at you. (*Looks round.*) It's warm in here, it's nice . . . This was the drawing-room then. Have I changed a lot?

KONSTANTIN. Yes, you have . . . You've lost weight, and

your eyes have got bigger. Nina, it's strange somehow to be seeing you. Why didn't you ever let me in? Why didn't you come sooner? I know you've been living here for almost a week . . . I've been coming every day, several times a day, and standing under your window like a beggar.

NINA. I was afraid you'd hate me. Every night I dream that you're looking at me and not recognising me. If only you knew what things had been like! I've been coming here from the moment I arrived . . . walking by the lake. I've been by your house many times, but I couldn't make up my mind to come in. Let's sit down.

They sit.

We'll sit and talk. Talk and talk. It's nice in here – it's warm, it's cosy . . . You hear the wind? It says in Turgenev somewhere: 'Lucky the man who on nights like these has a roof over his head and a warm corner.' I'm the seagull. No, that's not right. (*Rubs her forehead.*) What was I talking about? Oh, yes . . . Turgenev . . . 'And Lord help all homeless wanderers . . .' It's all right. (*Sobs.*)

KONSTANTIN. Nina, you're crying again . . . Nina!

NINA. It's all right – it's a relief . . . I haven't cried these two whole years. Then last night I went to look at the garden to see if our theatre was still there. And it is – it's been standing there all this time. I cried for the first time in two years, and I felt a weight lifting, I felt my heart clearing. You see? – I've stopped crying. (*Takes him by the hand.*) So, you've become a writer now . . . You're a writer – I'm an actress . . . We're launched upon the world, even us . . . I used to be full of joy in life, like a little child – I'd wake up in the morning and start singing – I loved you – I had dreams of glory . . . And now? First thing tomorrow morning I'm off to Yeletz – third class, with the peasants – and in Yeletz I shall have the more educated local businessmen pressing their attentions upon me. It's a rough trade, life!

KONSTANTIN. Why Yeletz?

NINA. I'm contracted for the entire winter season. It's time to be getting there.

KONSTANTIN. Nina, I've cursed you, I've hated you, I've torn up your letters and your photographs – but not a moment when I didn't know that I was bound to you, heart and soul, for all eternity. It's not within my power to cease loving you, Nina. From the moment I lost you and began to be published I've found my life unliveable – nothing but pain . . . It's as if my youth had suddenly been stripped from me – I feel I've been living in this world for ninety years. I say your name – I kiss the ground you've walked upon. Wherever I look I see your face – I see the tender smile that shone on me in the summer of my life . . .

NINA (*dismayed*). Why are you talking like this?

KONSTANTIN. I'm all alone. I've no one's affection to warm me – I'm as cold as the grave – and whatever I write, it's dry and stale and joyless. Stay here, Nina, I beg you, or else let me come with you!

NINA quickly puts on her hat and shawl.

KONSTANTIN. Nina, why? Nina, for the love of God . . .

He watches her put her things on. Pause.

NINA. My horses are at the gate. Don't come out – I'll find my own way . . . (*On the verge of tears.*) Give me some water.

KONSTANTIN (*gives her a drink of water*). Where are you going now?

NINA. Into town. (*Pause.*) Is your mother here?

KONSTANTIN. Yes, she is . . . Uncle was taken ill last Thursday and we wired her to come.

NINA. Why do you say you kissed the ground I walked upon? I ought to be put to death. (*Leans on the table.*) I'm so tired! If only I could rest . . . just rest! (*Raises her head.*) I'm the seagull . . . That's not right. I'm the actress. Yes!

Hears ARKADINA *and* TRIGORIN *laughing. Listens, then runs to the lefthand door and looks through the keyhole.*

He's here, too . . . (*Crosses back to* KONSTANTIN.) Yes, of course . . . Not that it matters . . . Of course, though . . . He didn't believe in the theatre – he did nothing but laugh at my ambitions – and gradually I stopped believing, too – I began to lose heart . . . Then there were the burdens of love – the jealousy, the perpetual anxiety for my little boy . . . I became a paltry thing, a nonentity – my acting lost all meaning . . . I didn't know what to do with my hands, I didn't know how to stand, I couldn't control my voice. You don't understand what it's like when you feel you're acting badly. I'm the seagull. No, that's not right . . . Do you remember – you shot a seagull? One day by chance a man comes along and sees her. And quite idly he destroys her . . . An idea for a short story . . . That's not right . . . (*Rubs her forehead.*) What was I talking about . . .? Acting, yes . . . I'm not like that now . . . I've become a real actress. I take pleasure in my performance – I delight in it. I'm in a state of intoxication up there – I feel I'm beautiful. And now, while I've been staying here, I've kept walking round – walking and walking, thinking and thinking – and I've had the feeling that with every day my spiritual strength has grown . . . I know now, Kostya, I understand now, that in our work – and it makes no difference whether we're acting or whether we're writing – the main thing is not the fame, not the glory, not all the things I used to dream of; it's the ability to endure. Learn to bear your cross; have faith. I have faith, and for me the pain is less. And when I think about my vocation, I'm not afraid of life.

KONSTANTIN (*sadly*). You've found your way – you know where you're going. While I'm still floundering in a chaos of dreams and images without knowing who or what it's all for. I've no faith, nor any idea where my vocation lies.

NINA (*listens*). Sh . . . I'm going. Goodbye. When I've become
a great actress come and see me perform. You promise? But
now . . . (*Presses his hand.*) It's late. I can scarcely stand . . .
I'm so tired, I'm so hungry . . .

KONSTANTIN. Stay here – I'll give you some supper . . .

NINA. No, no . . . Don't come out – I'll find my own way . . .
The horses are close by . . . So she's brought him with her?
Well, there we are – it makes no difference. Don't tell
Trigorin anything when you see him . . . I love him. I love
him even more than before . . . An idea for a short story . . .
I love him; I love him passionately; I love him to the point
of desperation. It was good before, Kostya! Do you
remember? Such a bright, warm, joyous, innocent life. Such
feelings. Feelings like graceful, delicate flowers . . . Do you
remember? (*Recites.*) 'Men and lions, partridges and eagles,
spiders, geese, and antlered stags, the unforthcoming fish
that dwelt beneath the waters, starfish and creatures invisible
to the naked eye; in short – all life, all life, all life, its dismal
round concluded, has guttered out. Thousands of centuries
have passed since any living creature walked the earth, and
this poor moon in vain lights up her lantern. In the meadows
the dawn cry of the crane is heard no more, and the May bugs
are silent in the lime groves . . .'

> *Embraces* KONSTANTIN *impulsively, and runs out through
> the glass door.*

KONSTANTIN (*after a pause*). Just so long as no one meets her
in the garden and then tells Mama. It might distress
Mama . . .

> *Over the next two minutes he silently tears up all his
> manuscripts and throws them under the desk, then opens the
> righthand door and goes out.*

DORN (*off, trying to open the lefthand door*). Odd. The door seems
to be locked . . .

He enters, and puts the armchair back in its place.

Obstacle race.

Enter ARKADINA *and* POLINA, *followed by* YAKOV, *bearing bottles and* MASHA, *then* SHAMRAYEV *and* TRIGORIN.

ARKADINA. Put the wine, and the beer for Boris Alekseyevich, on the table here. We're going to drink as we play. Do sit down, everyone.

POLINA (*to* YAKOV). Look sharp, now, and bring some tea as well. (*Lights the candles and sits down at the card-table.*)

SHAMRAYEV *takes* TRIGORIN *across to the cupboard.*

SHAMRAYEV. This is the thing I was telling you about earlier . . . (*Gets the stuffed seagull out of the cupboard.*) You asked me to have it done.

TRIGORIN (*looks at the seagull*). No recollection! (*After a moment's thought.*) No recollection!

A shot, off right. Everyone jumps.

ARKADINA (*alarmed*). What was that?

DORN. Nothing to worry about. Something in my medicine chest bursting, I expect. No cause for alarm.

He goes off through the righthand door, and a few moments later comes back in again.

Yes, that's what it was. A bottle of ether bursting. (*He hums to himself.*)

ARKADINA (*sitting down at the table*). Oh, it frightened me! It reminded me of the time when . . . (*Puts her hands over her face.*) I thought for a moment I was going to faint . . .

DORN (*leafing through a magazine; to* TRIGORIN). There was an article in here a couple of months back . . . From a correspondent in America, and I wanted to ask you, quite offhand . . . (*Puts an arm behind* TRIGORIN's *back and leads him away downstage.*) . . . this being a question that very much interests me . . . (*Lowers his voice.*) Get her out of here, will you. The fact is, he's shot himself . . .

CURTAIN